CONTEMPORARY'S

GED

TEST 5: MATHEMATICS

EXERCISE BOOK

CB

CONTEMPORARY BOOKS

a division of NTC/CONTEMPORARY PUBLISHING GROUP
Lincolnwood, Illinois USA

Writer: Robert Mitchell

ISBN: 0-8092-4545-0

Published by Contemporary Books,
a division of NTC/Contemporary Publishing Group, Inc.,
4255 West Touhy Avenue,
Lincolnwood (Chicago), Illinois 60712-1975 U.S.A.

1 2 3 4 5 6 7   DBH   35 34 32 31 30 29 28 27

Contents

Introduction

Welcome to Contemporary's *GED Test 5: Mathematics Exercise Book*. The ten chapters in this book will help you study for the GED Mathematics Test. They give you additional practice in the areas covered in our main GED mathematics textbook. Contemporary's *GED Test 5: Mathematics*. At the beginning of each chapter in this exercise book, you'll see references to *text pages*. Those pages refer to the instruction provided in the main GED math book. Refer to this book if you need a review before you work on the exercises.

This exercise book contains a pre-test and a practice test. Before you start to work on the exercises, it is a good idea to take the pre-test to help you determine the computation areas in which you may need more work. When you're finished with the exercises in the book, you can take the practice test. It is the same length and format as the actual GED Mathematics Test, and by completing the evaluation chart on page 92, you can see the areas in which you may need more work before you attempt the actual test.

The problems in each chapter of this book are divided into three parts. Part One is always a review of the basic computation issues. Part Two involves some more complex computation, such as multi-step problems, and includes some word problems as well. Part Three, labeled "GED Practice," provides multiple-choice word problems that represent the same level of difficulty that you will find on the actual GED Mathematics Test. It is in this section that you will practice the full range of problem-solving and computation skills that are important for success on the GED Mathematics Test.

THE GED MATHEMATICS TEST

Content Areas

The GED Mathematics Test includes 56 problems and can be broken down into these content areas:

- Arithmetic   50%
- Algebra   30%
- Geometry   20%

Types of Problems

All problems on the test are multiple-choice; you will be given five possible answer choices and asked to choose the correct one. Approximately one-third of the items on the test will be based on diagrams, charts, or graphs. Some of the questions will appear in "item sets"—short passages followed by two or more questions.

Some questions on the GED Math Test will not require you to do any computation; instead, you will have to choose the correct way to "set up" the problem in order to solve it. In other problems, you will be asked to determine what additional information is necessary to solve a problem. Still other problems will include an answer choice reading, "Not enough information is given." The first section of this exercise book, "Problem Solving with Whole Numbers," gives you plenty of instruction and practice with these types of problems.

Pre-Test

OVERVIEW OF COMPUTATION SKILLS

This pre-test will help you determine whether you need any review work in computation before you work on the word problems in this book. Work carefully through each problem, and use the evaluation chart on page 7 to see if you need review in any skill area.

Directions: Solve each problem as indicated.

1. $\begin{array}{r} 39 \\ + 28 \end{array}$

2. $\begin{array}{r} 3405 \\ + 986 \end{array}$

3. $\begin{array}{r} 87 \\ - 39 \end{array}$

4. $\begin{array}{r} 52 \\ \times 6 \end{array}$

5. $\begin{array}{r} 527 \\ \times 304 \end{array}$

6. $4\overline{)60}$

7. $8\overline{)856}$

8. $26\overline{)3484}$

9. $\begin{array}{r} 4.9 \\ + 2.4 \end{array}$

10. $\begin{array}{r} 12.5 \\ + 3.36 \end{array}$

11. $\begin{array}{r} 12.06 \\ - 4.87 \end{array}$

12. $\begin{array}{r} 8 \\ - 5.34 \end{array}$

13. $\begin{array}{r} 3.24 \\ \times 12 \end{array}$

14. $2.8\overline{)36.4}$

15. $\begin{array}{r} 9.81 \\ \times 3.7 \end{array}$

16. $.09\overline{)1.89}$

17. $\begin{array}{r} 2\frac{9}{16} \\ + 1\frac{8}{16} \end{array}$

18. $\begin{array}{r} 4\frac{7}{8} \\ + 1\frac{5}{16} \end{array}$

19. $\begin{array}{r} 1 \\ - \frac{2}{3} \end{array}$

20. $\begin{array}{r} 7\frac{1}{6} \\ - 3\frac{5}{6} \end{array}$

21. $\begin{array}{r} 12\frac{3}{8} \\ - 6\frac{3}{4} \end{array}$

22. $\frac{1}{3} \times \frac{3}{4}$

23. $2\frac{1}{4} \times 6$

24. $4\frac{3}{5} \times 3\frac{1}{3}$

25. $\frac{1}{2} \div \frac{1}{4}$

26. $1\frac{2}{3} \div \frac{1}{3}$

27. $4\frac{3}{8} \div 7$

28. $3\frac{3}{8} \div 2\frac{1}{2}$

29. $6 \div 2\frac{4}{5}$

Directions: Determine each number as indicated.

30. 30% of 60

31. 5.5% of 1200

32. $\frac{3}{4}$% of 28

33. 40% of what number is 52?

34. $33\frac{1}{3}$% of what number is 29?

ANSWERS ARE ON PAGE 5.

3

Directions: Determine each percent as indicated.

35. 14 is what percent of 70?

36. 330 is what percent of 220?

37. 1.25 is what percent of 25?

Directions: Solve each problem as indicated and simplify each answer.

38.   3 feet 8 inches
     × 4

39. $3\overline{)7\text{ gallons 2 quarts}}$

Directions: Solve each equation.

40. $x + 9 = 16$

41. $2y + 3 = y + 15$

42. $\frac{x}{8} = \frac{48}{128}$

43. $3(x - 5) = 2x$

Directions: Determine the value of each expression.

44. $2(9) - 4(3)$

45. $(2 + 3)(3 + 1)$

46. $-8 - (-7)$

47. $3^3 + 2^2$

48. $\sqrt{169}$

49.

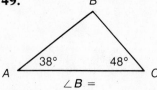

∠B =

50.

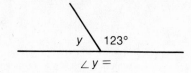

∠y =

ANSWERS ARE ON PAGE 6.

Pre-Test Answers

1.
$$\begin{array}{r} 39 \\ +\ 28 \\ \hline \mathbf{67} \end{array}$$

2.
$$\begin{array}{r} 3,405 \\ +\ \ \ 986 \\ \hline \mathbf{4,391} \end{array}$$

3.
$$\begin{array}{r} 87 \\ -\ 39 \\ \hline \mathbf{48} \end{array}$$

4.
$$\begin{array}{r} 52 \\ \times\ \ 6 \\ \hline \mathbf{312} \end{array}$$

5.
$$\begin{array}{r} 527 \\ \times\ 304 \\ \hline 2\ 108 \\ 158\ 10 \\ \hline \mathbf{160,208} \end{array}$$

6.
$$\begin{array}{r} 15 \\ 4\overline{)60} \\ 4 \\ \hline 20 \\ 20 \end{array}$$

7.
$$\begin{array}{r} \mathbf{107} \\ 8\overline{)856} \\ 8 \\ \hline 56 \\ 56 \end{array}$$

8.
$$\begin{array}{r} \mathbf{134} \\ 26\overline{)3,484} \\ 2\ 6 \\ \hline 88 \\ 78 \\ \hline 104 \\ 104 \end{array}$$

9.
$$\begin{array}{r} 4.9 \\ +\ 2.4 \\ \hline \mathbf{7.3} \end{array}$$

10.
$$\begin{array}{r} 12.5 \\ +\ \ 3.36 \\ \hline \mathbf{15.86} \end{array}$$

11.
$$\begin{array}{r} 12.06 \\ -\ 4.87 \\ \hline \mathbf{7.19} \end{array}$$

12.
$$\begin{array}{r} 8 \\ -\ 5.34 \\ \hline \mathbf{2.66} \end{array}$$

13.
$$\begin{array}{r} 3.24 \\ \times\ \ \ 12 \\ \hline 6\ 48 \\ 32\ 4 \\ \hline \mathbf{38.88} \end{array}$$

14.
$$\begin{array}{r} 1\ 3 \\ 2.8\overline{)36.4} \\ 28 \\ \hline 8\ 4 \\ 8\ 4 \end{array}$$

15.
$$\begin{array}{r} 9.81 \\ \times\ \ 3.7 \\ \hline 68\ 67 \\ 294\ 3 \\ \hline \mathbf{36.297} \end{array}$$

16.
$$\begin{array}{r} 21 \\ .09\overline{)1.89} \\ 1\ 8 \\ \hline 9 \\ 9 \end{array}$$

17.
$$\begin{array}{r} 2\frac{9}{16} \\ +\ 1\frac{8}{16} \\ \hline 3\frac{17}{16} = \mathbf{4\frac{1}{16}} \end{array}$$

18.
$$\begin{array}{r} 4\frac{7}{8} = 4\frac{14}{16} \\ +\ 1\frac{5}{16} = 1\frac{5}{16} \\ \hline 5\frac{19}{16} = \mathbf{6\frac{3}{16}} \end{array}$$

19.
$$\begin{array}{r} 1 = \frac{3}{3} \\ -\ \frac{2}{3} = \frac{2}{3} \\ \hline \mathbf{\frac{1}{3}} \end{array}$$

20.
$$\begin{array}{r} 7\frac{1}{6} = 6\frac{7}{6} \\ -\ 3\frac{5}{6} = 3\frac{5}{6} \\ \hline 3\frac{2}{6} = \mathbf{3\frac{1}{3}} \end{array}$$

21.
$$\begin{array}{r} 12\frac{3}{8} = 12\frac{3}{8} = 11\frac{11}{8} \\ -\ 6\frac{3}{4} = 6\frac{6}{8} = 6\frac{6}{8} \\ \hline \mathbf{5\frac{5}{8}} \end{array}$$

22. $\frac{1}{3} \times \frac{3}{4} = \frac{3}{12} = \mathbf{\frac{1}{4}}$

23. $2\frac{1}{4} \times 6$
$$= \frac{9}{4} \times \frac{6}{1} = \frac{27}{2} = \mathbf{13\frac{1}{2}}$$

24. $4\frac{3}{5} \times 3\frac{1}{3}$
$$= \frac{23}{5} \times \frac{10}{3} = \frac{46}{3} = \mathbf{15\frac{1}{3}}$$

25. $\frac{1}{2} \div \frac{1}{4}$
$$= \frac{1}{2} \times \frac{4}{1} = \frac{4}{2} = \mathbf{2}$$

26. $1\frac{2}{3} \div \frac{1}{3}$
$$= \frac{5}{3} \times \frac{3}{1} = \mathbf{5}$$

27. $4\frac{3}{8} \div 7$
$$= \frac{35}{8} \times \frac{1}{7} = \mathbf{\frac{5}{8}}$$

28. $3\frac{3}{8} \div 2\frac{1}{2}$
$$= \frac{27}{8} \div \frac{5}{2}$$
$$= \frac{27}{8} \times \frac{2}{5} = \frac{27}{20} = \mathbf{1\frac{7}{20}}$$

29. $6 \div 2\frac{4}{5}$
$$= \frac{6}{1} \div \frac{14}{5}$$
$$= \frac{6}{1} \times \frac{5}{14} = \frac{30}{14} = 2\frac{2}{14} = \mathbf{2\frac{1}{7}}$$

30. 30% of 60 = .3 × 60
$$\begin{array}{r} 60 \\ \times\ \ .3 \\ \hline 18.0 = \mathbf{18} \end{array}$$

31. 5.5% of 1200 = .055 × 1200
$$\begin{array}{r} 1200 \\ \times\ \ .055 \\ \hline 6\ 000 \\ 60\ 00 \\ \hline 66.000 = \mathbf{66} \end{array}$$

32. $\frac{3}{4}$% of 28 = .75% of 28
$$= .0075 \times 28$$
$$\begin{array}{r} 28 \\ \times .0075 \\ \hline 140 \\ 196 \\ \hline .2100 = \mathbf{.21} \end{array}$$

33. To find the number, divide 52 by .4 (40%).
$$\begin{array}{r} \mathbf{130.} \\ .4\overline{)520.} \\ 4 \\ \hline 12 \\ 12 \\ \hline 0 \end{array}$$

34. To find the number, divide 29 by $\frac{1}{3}$ ($33\frac{1}{3}\%$).

$29 \div \frac{1}{3}$

$= \frac{29}{1} \times \frac{3}{1} = \frac{87}{1} = \mathbf{87}$

35. To find the percent, divide the part by the whole.

$$\begin{array}{r} .2 = \mathbf{20\%} \\ 70\overline{)\,14.0} \\ \underline{14\,0} \end{array}$$

36. To find the percent, divide the part by the whole.

$$\begin{array}{r} 1.5 = \mathbf{150\%} \\ 220\overline{)\,330.0} \\ \underline{220} \\ 110\,0 \\ \underline{110\,0} \end{array}$$

37. To find the percent, divide the part by the whole.

$$\begin{array}{r} .05 \\ 25\overline{)\,1.25} \\ \underline{1\,25} \end{array}$$

38.
$$\begin{array}{r} 3 \text{ feet} \quad 8 \text{ inches} \\ \times \qquad\qquad 4 \\ \hline \end{array}$$
12 feet 32 inches = 12 feet + 2 feet 8 inches
= **14 feet 8 inches**

39.
$$\begin{array}{r} \mathbf{2\ gallons \quad 2\ quarts} \\ 3\overline{)\,7 \text{ gallons} \quad 2 \text{ quarts}} \end{array}$$

$\frac{6}{1}$ gallon $= \frac{4}{6}$ quarts
$\underline{6}$

40. $x + 9 = 16$

$x + 9 - 9 = 16 - 9$

$\mathbf{\mathit{x} = 7}$

41. $2y + 3 = y + 15$

$2y - y = 15 - 3$

$\mathbf{\mathit{y} = 12}$

42. $\frac{x}{8} = \frac{48}{128}$

$x = \frac{48}{128}(8) = \frac{384}{128} = \mathbf{3}$

43. $3(x - 5) = 2x$

$3x - 15 = 2x$

$3x - 2x = 15$

$\mathbf{\mathit{x} = 15}$

44. $2(9) - 4(3)$

$= 18 - 12$

$= \mathbf{6}$

45. $(2 + 3)(3 + 1)$

$= (5)(4)$

$= \mathbf{20}$

46. $-8 - (-7)$

$= -8 + 7$

$= \mathbf{-1}$

47. $3^3 + 2^2$

$= 27 + 4$

$= \mathbf{31}$

48. $\sqrt{169} = 13$

$$\begin{array}{r} \text{Check:} \quad 13 \\ \times\ 13 \\ \hline 39 \\ 13 \\ \hline \mathbf{169} \end{array}$$

49. $\angle A + \angle B + \angle C = 180°$

$\angle B = 180° - \angle A - \angle C$

$= 180° - 38° - 48°$

$= \mathbf{94°}$

50. $\angle Y + 123° = 180°$

$\angle Y = 180° - 123°$

$= \mathbf{57°}$

Pre-Test Evaluation Chart

Use the chart below to help you determine the computation areas in which you may need more work. Circle the number of any problem you got wrong. If you missed more than one or two in any skill area, refer to the appropriate pages in Contemporary's *Test 5: Mathematics* satellite text for review.

Skill Area	Item Number	Satellite Review Pages	Number Correct
Basic Operations with Whole Numbers	1, 2, 3, 4, 5, 6, 7, 8	11–19	_____/8
Adding and Subtracting Decimals	9, 10, 11, 12	60–63	_____/4
Multiplying and Dividing Decimals	13, 14, 15, 16	63–69	_____/4
Adding and Subtracting Fractions	17, 18, 19, 20, 21	89–99	_____/5
Multiplying and Dividing Fractions	22, 23, 24, 25, 26, 27, 28, 29	100–110	_____/8
Using Percents	30, 31, 32, 33, 34, 35, 36, 37	131–163	_____/8
Measurement	38, 39	165–175	_____/2
Algebra	40, 41, 42, 43, 44, 45, 46	195–221	_____/7
Geometry	47, 48, 49, 50	223–277	_____/4
		Total	_____/50

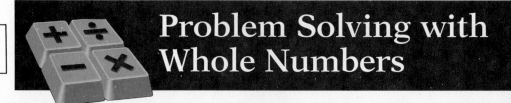

Problem Solving with Whole Numbers

FIVE STEPS TO PROBLEM SOLVING

The goal of the *GED Mathematics Exercise Book* is to help you develop and master problem-solving skills. This first chapter will give you practice in applying the five-step approach to solving word problems using whole numbers, and will introduce you to several kinds of problems that appear on the GED Mathematics Test.

The five-step approach to problem solving consists of these steps:

STEP 1. Find the question — what is being asked for?

STEP 2. Decide what information you need in order to answer the question.

STEP 3. Decide what arithmetic operation to use (addition, subtraction, multiplication, or division).

STEP 4. Do the arithmetic carefully, and check your work.

STEP 5. Make sure you answered the question asked and that your answer is sensible.

Directions: In each problem below, underline the necessary information: the numbers and labels (for example, pounds) needed to answer each question. Then use the necessary information and solve each problem.

1. At the beginning of his diet, Donald weighed 196 pounds. After 4 months of dieting, he lost more than 20 pounds, and his weight is now 175 pounds. How many pounds did Donald lose on this diet?

2. Everett earns $27,600 a year on his assembly job in an automobile plant. His wife earns $18,000 a year as a secretary in the same facility. How much does Everett earn in 3 months' time?

3. Andy sells used cars at Lee's Used Car Lot. During his worst sales month, Andy sold only 3 cars, but during his best month he sold 31. If overall he averages 12 sales per month, how many cars has Andy sold in the two years he has worked at Lee's?

4. While shopping at Better Buy Market, Cheryl bought 3 pounds of chicken, 5 pounds of beef, and 4 pounds of fish. What is the total weight of the fish and chicken that Cheryl bought?

5. Jeff bought five cases of oil with which to do his own oil changes. Each case contains 12 quarts. If he uses 4 quarts per oil change, how many oil changes can he make from the oil he has purchased?

ANSWERS ARE ON PAGE 93.

6. Jenny and her two sisters agreed to split the cost of lunch. If the bill includes sandwiches for $7.35, salads for $6.46, drinks for $4.80, and a sales tax of $.86, what is each sister's share?

7. While shopping at Apex Hardware, Wally bought a drill for $38.99 and a wrench for $8.88. What amount of change should Wally receive if he pays the clerk with three 20-dollar bills?

8. Donna had her car worked on at Ron's Auto Repair. Ron charged her a total of $126.50. His bill indicated a labor charge, a $68.00 charge for a new starter, and a $12.50 charge for new spark plugs. What amount did Ron charge for labor?

9. When Ken bought his two-year-old Ford, the odometer indicated 26,400 miles. During the first 6 months he owned the car, Ken drove an average of 1100 miles each month. The following 6 months, he drove an average of 1400 miles each month. After his first year of ownership, how many miles showed on the Ford's odometer?

10. On the way to the drive-in movie with his family, Stan bought a bag of oranges for $3.45, a half-dozen doughnuts for $1.50, and a six-pack of soft drinks for $2.89. If he wants to receive $10 change from the clerk, for how much should Stan write a check when paying for the groceries?

   (1) $7.09   **(2)** $7.84   **(3)** $10.00   **(4)** $17.84   **(5)** $170.84

11. There are 326 students and staff members at Highland View Elementary School. They include 139 girl students, 152 boy students, 4 custodians, 5 kitchen workers, and 6 office staff. If the remainder are teachers, how many teachers work at Highland View?

   (1) 18   **(2)** 20   **(3)** 36   **(4)** 306   **(5)** 318

12. At a Memorial Day sale, Jay bought 4 shirts on sale for $2.00 off their regular price of $8.99, and 6 pairs of socks on sale for $1.00 off their regular price of $1.98. How much did these purchases cost Jay?

   (1) $5.88   **(2)** $11.88   **(3)** $27.96   **(4)** $33.84   **(5)** $41.84

13. During a special "Wholesale Prices Only" sale at the local Food Warehouse, Chris bought 6 cases of canned corn, 4 cases of canned peas, 3 cases of canned mixed vegetables, and 4 cases of mixed fruit. If each case contains 24 cans, how many cans of vegetables did Chris buy?

   (1) 13   **(2)** 31   **(3)** 308   **(4)** 309   **(5)** 312

14. To purchase her new couch, Mrs. Dahl paid $150 down and agreed to make monthly payments of $35.42 for 1 year. Rounded to the nearest dollar, how much will Mrs. Dahl pay for her couch?

   (1) $575   **(2)** $425   **(3)** $275   **(4)** $186   **(5)** $185

ANSWERS ARE ON PAGE 93.

INSUFFICIENT INFORMATION

On the GED Mathematics Test, some problems do not give enough information to enable you to find a solution. Following are examples that illustrate the two ways that the few GED problems of this type will appear.

EXAMPLE A: Joan buys 4 bottles of shampoo during a coupon sale at the Variety Store. Her coupon reads "Shampoo: 1st 2 bottles for $1.29 each, others at regular price." How much must Joan pay for the 4 bottles?

    (1) $2.58
    (2) $5.16
    (3) $6.58
    (4) $7.05
    (5) Not enough information is given.

The correct answer choice is (5). To solve the problem, you must know the regular price of the shampoo, and the problem does not give you this number. Joan pays the regular price for two of the four bottles. She pays $1.29 each for only the first two bottles.

When you see a question where answer choice 5 is "Not enough information is given," be careful. Many times, this answer choice will not be the correct one! Before choosing (5), Not enough information is given, as the answer, be sure you can clearly identify what information is actually missing from the problem. Only by doing this can you be sure that choice (5) is correct.

EXAMPLE B: Joan buys 4 bottles of shampoo during a coupon sale at the Variety Store. Her coupon reads "Shampoo: 1st 2 bottles for $1.29 each, others at regular price." What more do you need to know to find out how much Joan paid for the 4 bottles?

    (1) the size of each bottle
    (2) the total cost of the first two bottles
    (3) the regular price of the shampoo
    (4) the usual sale price of the shampoo
    (5) the expiration date of the coupon

In this example, answer choice 3 is correct. Notice that, unlike Example A, the question in Example B lets you know that not enough information is given. In this type of problem you must identify the missing information from a list of choices. Being able to identify missing information is the main skill to learn in correctly answering GED questions like these examples.

Directions: In each problem below, identify what information you need in order to answer the question.

1. Each Monday, Wednesday, and Friday, Brenda practices the piano for 30 minutes, concentrating on learning new pieces. Each Tuesday and Thursday, she spends her practice time reviewing pieces she has memorized. In an average 5-day week, how many total minutes does Brenda practice piano?

    Missing information:

2. Gina sent a bag of apples to her daughter's kindergarten class. If she sent 24 apples and each of the 16 girls, each boy, and the teacher ate 1 apple, how many apples were left over?

    Missing information:

3. Monday through Friday from 1:00 P.M. to 4:00 P.M. Carol and Sandy work as waitresses in the Pancake House. They each earn $4.75 an hour and, as part of their income, they evenly split all the tips they receive. During a week when Sandy took in $62 in tips from the tables she worked on, how much was her weekly income?

    Missing information:

4. To help finance the purchase of her new car, Diana borrowed $12,000 from her credit union. She must pay the loan back in monthly payments of $367.50. When she has totally repaid the loan, how much money will she actually have paid out for the car?

    Missing information:

5. On the first day of a cross-country trip, Mr. Johns drove at an average speed of 50 miles per hour for 4 hours of morning driving. After stopping for lunch at 12:00 noon, he drove until 5:00 that evening, again averaging 50 miles per hour. How many miles did Mr. Johns drive that first day of the trip?

    Missing information:

6. When the price of fresh salmon steak was reduced from $6.85 per pound, Mrs. Rogers bought 6 pounds. She also bought 3 pounds of chicken on sale for $1.29 per pound. Determine how much Mrs. Rogers spend on these two items.

    Missing information:

7. As part of his diet, Warren counts the calories of the foods he eats. How many calories will he consume in a lunch that consists of a 425-calorie hamburger, a 245-calorie serving of french fries, and a glass of milk?

    Missing information:

8. Carlin and several friends agree to split the cost of a pizza dinner. The bill includes 1 large pizza for $14.95, 4 salads for $5.80, 4 beers for $4.80, and a sales tax of $1.26. What is Carlin's share of this bill?

    Missing information:

ANSWERS ARE ON PAGE 93.

MEAN, MEDIAN, & NUMBER SERIES

The problems in this section check your knowledge of three topics dealing with number relationships: mean, median, and number series.

- *Mean* is another word for average. To find an average of a group of values you add them together and then divide the sum by the number of numbers added.

- The *median* is simply the middle value of a group of values. For an even number of values, the median is the average of the two middle values.

- A *number series* is a list of values that show a special order or pattern. Questions usually ask you to identify a pattern and to extend a given series.

Directions: Solve each problem below.

1. Derek is mailing two packages, one weighing 8 pounds and one weighing 14 pounds. Find the average weight of these packages.

2. Bill, Sal, and Robert work together at Pine City Lumber. Determine their average salary if Bill's salary is $8 per hour, Sal's is $9 per hour, and Robert's is $13 per hour.

3. The Lakeridge High Huskies scored 49, 45, and 53 points in their first three basketball games of the season. What is their mean score for these games?

4. During league play, Emma bowled games of 136, 129, 141, and 130. Find Emma's average score for these league games.

5. Each year, Jan's highest heating bills occur during November, December, January, and February. If her monthly bills this year were $176.50, $188.93, $207.58, and $196.75, respectively, determine the average monthly amount she paid for heat during these months.

6. On Monday, Wednesday, and Friday, Lucian gets up at 6:00 A.M. On Tuesdays he is up at 8:00 A.M., and Thursdays he sleeps until 9:00 A.M. For these five days, what is the average time Lucian gets up?

7. Mrs. Hill has 23 students in her 3rd-grade class. During one winter week, when kids had colds, the enrollment was as shown at right. During that week, what was the average number of kids absent per day?

Day	Enrollment
Monday	14
Tuesday	17
Wednesday	15
Thursday	16
Friday	18

8. On three practice math tests of 56 questions each, Marian had scores of 38, 41, and 47. If a score of 30 is necessary to pass each test, how many points above the passing score is Marian's average score?

9. During the months of May, June, and July, Avril drove 1200, 1350, and 1440 miles, respectively. How many miles did Avril average per month during these months?

10. Find the median in the following set of amounts: $34, $38, $41, $54, and $89.

11. Determine the median of the following temperatures: 80°F, 87°F, 97°F, and 102°F.

ANSWERS ARE ON PAGE 93.

12. Find the median age of Charlie's children: Krista, age 7; Debbie, age 10; Kira, age 12; and Lindsay, age 15.

13. For the three attendance figures shown at right, how much larger is the median than the mean?

Attendance Record	
Game 1	4,530
Game 2	3,920
Game 3	4,750

14. Choose the expression below that best describes how the following series is changing: 6, 12, 9, 15, 12, 18, 15 . . . .

(1) add 6

(2) subtract 3

(3) add 4, subtract 3

(4) add 6, subtract 3

(5) add 3, subtract 6

15. Find the next term in the series 1, 2, 4, 8, 16 . . . .

16. Find the sixth term in the series 150, 146, 142, 138 . . . .

17. Find the missing fourth term in the series 1, 3, 6, ____, 15 . . . .

18. Each month Buzz puts part of his earnings in his savings account, a record of which is shown at right. If he continues to save at the same rate, how much will be in his account at the end of May?

Date	Savings
Feb. 29	$455
March 31	$537
April 30	$619
May 31	____

19. While on a 1200 calorie a day diet, Nancy's weight dropped steadily as shown in the table at right. If she stays on this diet and loses weight at the same rate, how much more weight can she expect to lose in the next four months?

Date	Weight
June 1	164
July 1	159
Aug. 1	154

20. Jason found part of a bus schedule shown at right. The afternoon departure times follow the same pattern as the morning times. If it is now Wednesday at 12:15 P.M., what time can Jason expect the next bus to leave the Walnut Street stop?

BUS SCHEDULE

Wednesday — Walnut Street
Departure Times

10:00 A.M.
10:25 A.M.
10:35 A.M.
11:00 A.M.
11:10 A.M.
11:35 A.M.
11:45 A.M.
12:10 P.M.

ANSWERS ARE ON PAGE 93.

SET-UP QUESTIONS

In some questions on the GED Mathematics Test, you do not actually solve a problem in the usual way. You are not asked to find a numerical answer. Instead, you are asked to choose an expression that—if evaluated—would give the correct solution. Set-up questions check your understanding of the question being asked and check your knowledge of the properties of numbers.

> If Sarah works eighteen hours one week at $5.50 per hour, and her husband works thirty hours at twice that wage, which of the following expressions tells the total amount husband and wife earned that week?
>
> **(1)** $(30 + 18)5.50$
> **(2)** $(30 + 18)(5.50 + 11.00)$
> **(3)** $(18 \times 5.50)(30 \times 11.00)$
> **(4)** $(18 \times 5.50) + (30 \times 11.00)$
> **(5)** $(18 + 5.50)(30 + 11.00)$

Choice (4) shows the correct way to set up this problem. To get the right answer, you would multiply Sarah's hours by her hourly wage and add this number to the product of her husband's hours and his hourly wage.

Directions: Solve each set-up question below. The first four questions check your knowledge of the properties of numbers.

1. Which of the following expressions has the same value as $(3)(4 + 5)$?

   (1) $12 + 15$ **(2)** $12 + 5$ **(3)** $3 + 9$ **(4)** $(3)(45)$ **(5)** $34 + 5$

2. Which of the following expressions has the same value as $(20)(8) - \frac{6}{3}$?

   (1) $\frac{(160 - 6)}{3}$ **(2)** $\frac{(160 - 48)}{3}$ **(3)** $\frac{160 - 48}{3}$ **(4)** $160 - 2$ **(5)** $160 + 2$

3. Which of the following expressions has the same value as $(8)(7 - 4)$?

   (1) $(8)(7) - (7)(4)$

   (2) $(8)(7) - (8)(4)$

   (3) $(8)(7) - 4$

   (4) $(8)(7) - \frac{8}{4}$

   (5) $(8)(7) - 3$

4. Which of the following expressions has the same value as $(5)(2) + (5)(6)$?

   (1) $(5 + 2)(5 + 6)$
   (2) $(5 + 5)(2 + 6)$
   (3) $(5)(2) + (2)(6)$
   (4) $(5)(2) + 6$
   (5) $(5)(2 + 6)$

5. During May, Henry sold 250 lawn mowers priced at $189. During June, he sold 82 more at the same price. Which expression represents the dollar amount of lawn mower sales Henry made during these two months?

   (1) $250 - 82$
   (2) $250 + 82$
   (3) $(189)(250 + 82)$
   (4) $(189)(250 - 82)$
   (5) $(189)(250)(82)$

ANSWERS ARE ON PAGE 93.

6. Shellie works 5 hours each Monday, Wednesday, and Friday on her part-time job at Happy Burgers. On Tuesdays and Thursdays, she works 4 hours each day. Which expression represents the total number of hours Shellie works each week on her part-time job?

   (1) $(5)(3) + (4)(2)$
   (2) $(5)(2) + (4)(3)$
   (3) $(5)(4) + (3)(2)$
   (4) $(5 + 4)(3 + 2)$
   (5) $(5 + 3)(4 + 2)$

7. Mickey can lay 46 floor tiles each hour, and his assistant Elvin can lay 41 each hour. If both men are working, which expression tells how many floor tiles they can lay in 4 hours?

   (1) $(4)(46) - (4)(41)$
   (2) $\frac{(46 - 41)}{4}$
   (3) $\frac{(46 + 41)}{4}$
   (4) $(4)(46 - 41)$
   (5) $(4)(46 + 41)$

8. The three deductions withheld from Floyd's pay each month are $245 for federal tax, $68 for social security, and $42 for medical insurance. If Floyd's gross pay is $1325, which expression represents his take-home pay?

   (1) $1325 - (245 - 68 - 42)$
   (2) $1325 + (245 + 68 + 42)$
   (3) $1325 - (245 + 68 + 42)$
   (4) $(245 - 68 - 42) + 1325$
   (5) $(245 + 68 + 42) - 1325$

9. Shown at right is a 5-month record of the amount of gasoline Adele used after beginning her new job. Which expression represents the average number of gallons of gas she used per month during the first three months of the year?

Monthly Gas Use	
Month	**Gallons**
Jan.	150
Feb.	162
March	148
April	166
May	173

   (1) $\frac{(150 + 162 + 148 + 166 + 173)}{3}$
   (2) $\frac{(150 + 162 + 148 + 166 + 173)}{5}$
   (3) $\frac{(150 + 162 + 148)}{2}$
   (4) $\frac{(150 + 162 + 148)}{3}$
   (5) $\frac{(150 + 162 + 148)}{5}$

10. Carmen types at a rate of 54 words per minute. If an average page contains 640 words, which expression tells the number of minutes it will take Carmen to type 230 pages of manuscript?

   (1) $(230)(640)(54)$
   (2) $\frac{(230)(54)}{640}$
   (3) $\frac{(640)(54)}{230}$
   (4) $\frac{(230)(640)}{54}$
   (5) $\frac{230}{(640)(54)}$

ANSWERS ARE ON PAGE 93.

11. Al, a baker, started the morning with 60 pounds of dough. After using 42 pounds of dough to make bread, he divided the remaining dough into 50 equal portions to make apple turnovers. Which expression tells how much dough Al used to make each turnover?

(1) $\dfrac{(60-50)}{42}$ **(2)** $\dfrac{(60-42)}{50}$ **(3)** $\dfrac{(60+50)}{42}$ **(4)** $\dfrac{(60+42)}{50}$ **(5)** $\dfrac{(50-42)}{60}$

12. For use in her kindergarten class, Pam bought a box of 130 crayons. After she divided the crayons equally among her eight students, she had two left over. She gave these two to Sally because Sally was most apt to break crayons. Which expression tells how many crayons Pam gave Sally?

(1) $\dfrac{(130+2)}{8}$ **(2)** $\dfrac{(130-2)}{8}$ **(3)** $\dfrac{130}{8}+\dfrac{8}{2}$ **(4)** $\dfrac{(130-2)}{8}+2$ **(5)** $\dfrac{130}{8}-2$

ANSWERS ARE ON PAGE 94.

ITEM SETS

An item set is a group of two or more questions that are based on the same short passage or on a graph, table, or drawing. Questions that are part of an item set are not more difficult than other questions on the GED. However, because of the additional information presented, you must be especially careful to choose only the specific information needed to answer each question.

Questions 1–4 are based on the following passage.

> On the first day of her vacation, Gloria used 14 gallons of gas driving the 440 miles between Emory and Eagle Point. The next day she used 12 gallons driving the remaining 364 miles to San Francisco. During the three days she was in San Francisco, Gloria used 7 gallons of gas and drove a total of 129 miles. Her mileage and gas usage on the way home were the same as on the first two days of the trip.

1. How many gallons of gas did Gloria use on the 7 days of her vacation?

2. How many total miles did Gloria drive on the 7 days of her vacation?

3. How many more miles did Gloria drive on the second day of her vacation than on the fourth day?

   (1) 76   **(4)** 398
   (2) 235   **(5)** Not enough information is given.
   (3) 320

4. What was the average number of miles Gloria drove each day during the 4 days she traveled to and from San Francisco?

   (1) 76   **(4)** 804
   (2) 201   **(5)** Not enough information is given.
   (3) 402

ANSWERS ARE ON PAGE 94.

Questions 5–8 refer to the following situation.

Ruben is trying to decide where to take his two children for hamburgers. Happy Mealtime offers children's burgers for $1.25. French fries are $.89 per child, and a soft drink or milk is an additional $.75. Ruben's meal at Happy Mealtime would cost $2.75. Burger Palace offers a child's Palace Special for $2.45. The special includes a burger, fries, and a soft drink or milk. Ruben's meal would cost $3.49 at Burger Palace.

5. If each child has a burger, fries, and milk, how much would Ruben spend for his two children at Happy Mealtime?

6. How much more would Ruben's own meal cost at Burger Palace than at Happy Mealtime?

7. How much could Ruben save on the cost of his children's meals of burgers, fries, and milk if they went to Burger Palace rather than to Happy Mealtime?

   (1) $.44   **(4)** $1.18
   (2) $.88   **(5)** Not enough information is given.
   (3) $1.04

8. To the nearest dollar, how much would Ruben pay to buy only burgers and fries for his children at Burger Palace, and not get them Palace Specials?

   (1) $2.00   **(4)** $5.00
   (2) $3.00   **(5)** Not enough information is given.
   (3) $4.00

Questions 9–11 are based on the following drawing.

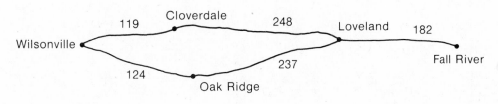

All distances are in miles.

9. What is the total distance from Wilsonville to Fall River on the route that goes through Oak Ridge?

10. What is the average distance of the two routes that go between Wilsonville and Loveland?

11. To determine whether the route through Cloverdale or the one through Oak Ridge gives the shortest distance between Wilsonville and Fall River, which of the following distances is *not* needed?

   (1) 119   **(2)** 248   **(3)** 124   **(4)** 237   **(5)** 182

ANSWERS ARE ON PAGE 94.

Decimals

PART ONE

1. Write a decimal to represent the part of the divided figure that is shaded at right.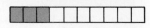

2. Write a decimal to represent the part of the large divided square that is shaded at right.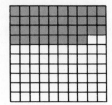

3. How many decimal places are in the number 23.042?

4. Express the number 5.134 in words.

5. Arrange the following numbers in order, writing the smallest number at the left, then the next largest, and so on:
   .0423, 40.23, .4023, 4.023

6. Round 18.0235 to the nearest thousandth.

7. Add 4.06 and 3.1.

8. Subtract eighty-nine cents from five dollars.

9. Subtract 2.04 from 4.173.

10. Subtract 1.34 from 6.2.

11. Multiply 1.03 by 6.

12. Multiply 4.25 by 2.6.

13. Divide 5.64 by 3.

14. Divide 20.5 by .05.

15. Spending $22.86 at Shopper's Market and $18.97 at Safeway, how much in all did Vicki spend?

16. Howard has 2 quarters, 3 nickels, 1 dime, and 4 pennies in his pocket. What total amount of change does he have?

17. Before Marge had it tuned up, her car averaged 21.6 miles per gallon. After the tune-up, the car's mileage increased by 3.7 miles per gallon. What mileage does Marge's car get now?

18. The area of the state is Illinois is 56.4 thousand square miles, while the area of Ohio is 41.22 thousand square miles. By how many thousand square miles is Illinois larger than Ohio?

ANSWERS ARE ON PAGE 94.

19. Radio station KFLO broadcasts at a frequency of 96.6 megahertz (MHz), and station KRUN broadcasts at a frequency of 78.9 MHz. How many MHz separate the frequencies at which these two FM stations broadcast?

20. Between May 15 and July 1, Todd's batting average held steady at .386. By July 31, though, his average had fallen by .136. Determine Todd's batting average at the end of July.

21. As shown at right, how much longer are the nails in bin A than the nails in bin B?

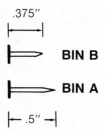

22. The new Jura Super Ski measures 2.14 meters in length. This is .08 meters longer than last year's Super model. Use this information to find the length of last year's Super model.

23. To smooth the surface of a solid oak table, Hal sanded .086 inch off the surface. If the table top was .75 inch thick before it was sanded, how thick is it now?

24. For each suit he sells for $298.00, Barry makes a profit of $97.45. What are Barry's total costs on each $298.00 suit?

25. Determine the weight of a case of corn in which each of the 24 cans of corn weighs 1.75 pounds.

26. Earning $8.64 for each overtime hour he works, how much can Toby earn working 3.5 hours of overtime Saturday morning?

27. Marie bought 3.8 pounds of beef for $14.63. At this rate, what price is Marie paying per pound?

28. Aaron and his two brothers agreed to split the cost of breakfast evenly. If the bill comes to $13.89, what is Aaron's share?

29. While traveling to Yellowstone National Park, the Moore family drove 780 miles on 32.5 gallons of gas. Determine how far on the average the Moores traveled on each gallon.

30. According to the picture at right, how much heavier is the larger jar of imported jam than the smaller jar?

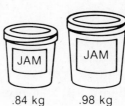

ANSWERS ARE ON PAGE 94.

PART TWO

1. For a total weight of less than 10 pounds, Marie can save postage by mailing several gifts in a single large box. What is the total weight of Marie's box of 3 presents if the empty box weighs .4 pound and the gifts weigh 1.25 pounds, 2.8 pounds, and 4.375 pounds?

2. In Scott's backpack are extra clothing weighing 3.2 pounds, cooking utensils weighing 4.7 pounds, and food supplies weighing 7.6 pounds. If Scott's pack weighs 2.3 pounds when empty, how much does it weigh with these contents?

3. Out of a county budget of 22.4 million dollars, 3.96 million goes to youth development programs, 1.8 million goes to county health services, and 2.43 million goes to handicapped services. How much of the total budget remains after money for youth development and handicapped services is taken out?

4. Chicken dark meat contains 7.3 grams of fat per 6-ounce serving, while an equal serving of chicken light meat contains 4 grams of fat. Ham, for comparison, contains 52.13 grams of fat per 6-ounce serving. How many more grams of fat are in 6 ounces of ham than in 6 ounces of chicken dark meat?

5. Ernie lives 7.8 miles away from his work. If his daughter's school is halfway between his house and his workplace, how many miles is the school from Ernie's home?

   (1) 2.6　　(2) 3.1　　(3) 3.6　　(4) 3.9　　(5) 4.2

6. Zack worked for 6.75 hours at an overtime rate of $9.51 per hour, 1.5 times his normal hourly rate of $6.34. To the nearest penny, how much did Zack earn for this work?

   (1) $42.80　　　　　　(4) $64.19
   (2) $49.40　　　　　　(5) Not enough information is given.
   (3) $57.53

7. Jack's Fill Up gives a $1.00 cash discount for any gasoline purchase over $12.00. How much would 15 gallons of gas cost at Jack's if the pump price per gallon is $1.499 and the customer pays cash?

   (1) $20.15　　　　　　(4) $22.49
   (2) $21.35　　　　　　(5) Not enough information is given.
   (3) $21.49

8. Roger earns $7.00 per hour. To the nearest dollar, how much can Roger earn in the 22 working days in the month of May if his work day averages 7 hours and he works 3 part-day overtime shifts for which he earns $10.50 per hour?

   (1) $1010　　　　　　(4) $1175
   (2) $1080　　　　　　(5) Not enough information is given.
   (3) $1110

9. There are 91.44 centimeters in one yard (36 inches). To the nearest tenth centimeter, determine how many centimeters are in one inch.

   (1) 2.2　　(2) 2.3　　(3) 2.4　　(4) 2.5　　(5) 2.6

ANSWERS ARE ON PAGE 94.

10. Referring to the table at right, how much more does the heaviest can of imported fruit cost than the lightest can?

(1) $1.06
(2) $1.12
(3) $1.17
(4) $1.23
(5) $1.29

IMPORTED MIXED FRUIT SALE	
(prices vary with manufacturer)	
Size	Price
Brand A 4.35 kg	$4.35
Brand B 4.0 kg	$5.06
Brand C 6.5 kg	$7.45
Brand D 6.81 kg	$6.12

ANSWERS ARE ON PAGE 94.

GED Practice
PART THREE

1. The scores of the first three games of the Linfield High School basketball team are shown at right. To the nearest tenth of a point, what is Linfield's average score for these three games?

(1) 54.6
(2) 55.4
(3) 56.3
(4) 57.8
(5) 59.2

Linfield Basketball Scores	
Game 1	57
Game 2	49
Game 3	63

2. Bill's calculator displays a maximum of 8 digits of an answer, and it does not display unnecessary zeros. If Bill divides 160 by 3 on his calculator, what answer will be displayed?

(1) 5.3
(2) 53.3
(3) 53.30
(4) 53.300000
(5) 53.333333

3. The prices of the Fun with Bikes rental shop are shown at right. What would be the minimum cost of renting a bike for six straight hours?

(1) $4.25
(2) $5.38
(3) $6.95
(4) $7.85
(5) $8.10

FUN WITH BIKES	
Hourly rate	$1.35
4-hour rate	$4.25
Daily rate	$7.85

4. At Twin Trees Builders' Supply, the prices of 4-foot-by-8-foot sheets of $\frac{1}{2}$-inch-thick plywood are shown at right. Which expression represents the cost of buying 3 Grade A sheets and 2 Grade B sheets?

(1) (2)(21.45) + (3)(24.65)
(2) (2)(24.65) + (3)(29.95)
(3) (2)(29.95) + (3)(24.65)
(4) (2 + 3)(24.65 + 29.95)
(5) (2 + 3)(29.95 + 24.65)

TWIN TREES LUMBER PRICES	
4' x 8' $\frac{1}{2}$-in plywood	
Grade A	$29.95
Grade B	$24.65
Grade C	$21.45

ANSWERS ARE ON PAGE 94.

5. As shown in the drawing at right, on a 1.125-inch bolt are 4 washers, each .0625 inch thick. What is the length of the bolt that is still uncovered?

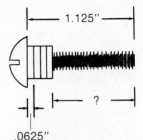

(1) .25 inch
(2) .5 inch
(3) .625 inch
(4) .875 inch
(5) 1.0625 inches

6. Shown below is a 6-meter-long pipe that Dean is going to cut into 7 pieces. First he will cut off a piece 2.8 meters long, and then he will cut the remaining piece into 6 pieces of equal length. Which expression represents the length of each of these shorter pieces?

(1) $\frac{(6-2.8)}{7}$

(2) $\frac{(6-2.8)}{6}$

(3) $(6-2.8)(7)$

(4) $\frac{(7-2.8)}{6}$

(5) $(6-2.8)(6)$

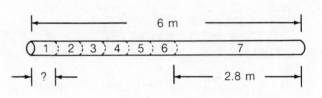

7. Three bolts are shown at right. Together with this drawing, what additional information would enable you to determine the average length of these three bolts?

A. the length of bolt B
B. the difference in the lengths of bolt A and bolt C
C. the length of bolt C

(1) A only   (4) A or B
(2) B only   (5) A or C
(3) C only

8. Peggy is placing library books on a shelf that measures 94 inches wide. She will shelve 64 books of average width 1.2 inches. In the space that is left over, she will shelve as many 2-inch-wide books as will fit. How many of these wider books will there be room for?

(1) 5   (2) 6   (3) 7   (4) 8   (5) 9

9. A 5-hour record of Tina's temperature is shown at right. To the nearest tenth of a degree, what was Tina's average temperature during this 5-hour period?

(1) 103.0°F
(2) 103.1°F
(3) 103.2°F
(4) 103.3°F
(5) 103.4°F

Record of Tina's Temperature	
1st hour	104.7°F
2nd hour	103.9°F
3rd hour	102.8°F
4th hour	102.4°F
5th hour	101.9°F

ANSWERS ARE ON PAGE 94.

10. At his garden shop, Louis sells topsoil by the ton. On Saturday he sold four pickup loads of topsoil as shown below:

Load A = .629 ton
Load B = .714 ton
Load C = .709 ton
Load D = .68 ton

Which sequence lists these four loads from heaviest to lightest?

(1) B, C, D, A   **(4)** C, D, A, B
(2) C, A, D, B   **(5)** B, C, A, D
(3) B, D, C, A

Questions 11–13 refer to the following situation.

In Anderson the price of electric power is $.0856 per kilowatt-hour. During the month of December, the Jenson family used 2750 kilowatt-hours of electric power. In December of the previous year, the Jensons had used more electricity than they used this December, but the rate they had paid then was only $.074 per kilowatt-hour.

11. During this December, what amount did the Jenson family pay for electric power?

(1) $211.90   **(2)** $215.30   **(3)** $225.80   **(4)** $235.40   **(5)** $242.60

12. How much more did the Jensons pay for each kilowatt-hour of electricity this December than they had paid for December of the previous year?

(1) $.01   **(2)** $.0104   **(3)** $.0116   **(4)** $.0124   **(5)** $.013

13. If the Jensons' electric bill last December had been $209.79, how many kilowatt-hours of electricity had they used that month?

(1) 2760   **(2)** 2835   **(3)** 2890   **(4)** 2935   **(5)** 3125

ANSWERS ARE ON PAGE 94.

Fractions

PART ONE

1. Reduce $\frac{8}{20}$ to lowest terms.

2. Write $\frac{14}{3}$ as a mixed number.

3. Write $\frac{20}{8}$ as a mixed number and reduce to lowest terms.

4. Find the sum of $4\frac{2}{3}$ and $2\frac{1}{3}$.

5. Subtract $2\frac{3}{5}$ from 7.

6. Add $4\frac{5}{6}$ and $2\frac{3}{8}$.

7. Multiply $\frac{5}{6}$ by $\frac{3}{4}$.

8. Write $3\frac{7}{8}$ as an improper fraction.

9. Multiply 7 by $3\frac{3}{4}$.

10. Find the product of $5\frac{1}{2}$ times $2\frac{2}{3}$.

11. Divide $\frac{15}{16}$ by $\frac{3}{8}$.

12. Divide $2\frac{3}{4}$ by $4\frac{1}{3}$.

13. Write .375 as a fraction and reduce to lowest terms.

14. Express $\frac{6}{25}$ as a decimal.

15. Which of the following is larger: $\frac{3}{7}$ or $\frac{4}{9}$?

Questions 16–17 are based on the measuring cup shown at right.

16. What fraction of the measuring cup is filled with water?

17. What fraction of the measuring cup is empty?

18. In an unusual April snowstorm in Redmond, $5\frac{1}{2}$ inches of snow fell Saturday, and an additional $4\frac{7}{8}$ inches fell on Sunday. Determine the total depth of snow that fell.

19. During the last special election, $\frac{9}{16}$ of the voters cast votes in favor of the measure on the lottery, and $\frac{1}{4}$ voted against it. By what fraction of the people voting did votes in favor of the measure exceed the votes against it?

20. From a bolt of $12\frac{1}{2}$ yards of cloth, a clerk cut off a piece measuring $4\frac{2}{3}$ yards. What length of cloth was left on the bolt?

ANSWERS ARE ON PAGE 95.

21. What is the difference in length between the two bolts shown in the drawing at right?

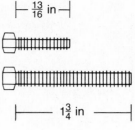

22. Seven-eighths of the homes on Parkway Drive have two-car garages. How many of the 56 homes along Parkway Drive have two-car garages?

23. If one cubic foot holds $7\frac{1}{2}$ gallons, how many gallons of gasoline does it take to fill a tank that has a volume of 3 cubic feet?

24. As shown in the drawing below, what fraction of the distance between Kim's house and the park is the distance between Kim's house and her school?

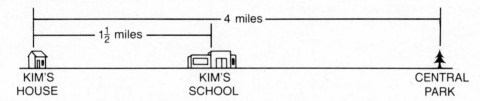

25. Comparing the two nails shown at right, what fraction of the length of the longer nail is the length of the shorter nail?

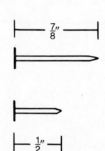

ANSWERS FOR PART ONE BEGIN ON PAGE 95.

PART TWO

1. To connect the hot-water supply to the faucet, Doug is using a flexible tube that is $18\frac{3}{4}$ inches long. If each of the two end connectors adds an additional $\frac{7}{16}$ inch to the tube, what maximum distance can this tube reach?

2. Katie jogs three days each week. What is her total weekly mileage if she jogs $4\frac{1}{2}$ miles on Monday, $3\frac{1}{4}$ miles on Wednesday, and $5\frac{7}{8}$ miles on Friday?

3. The Hickmans spend $\frac{1}{4}$ of their monthly income on rent, $\frac{5}{24}$ on food, $\frac{1}{8}$ on transportation, and $\frac{1}{6}$ on electricity. What total fraction of their income do the Hickmans use for these 4 expenses?

4. If the Lewis family spends $\frac{3}{8}$ of its total monthly income on rent and $\frac{1}{5}$ on car payments, what fraction of its income remains to cover other expenses?

ANSWERS ARE ON PAGE 95.

5. Between her 4th and 5th birthdays, Gena grew $2\frac{5}{8}$ inches. Between her 5th and 6th birthdays, she grew $3\frac{1}{16}$ inches. How much more did Gena grow when she was 5 years old than when she was 4?

6. Three-fifths of the 25 students in Mrs. Miles's 3rd-grade class are girls. How many boys are in this class?

7. Leo, a plumber, cut $3\frac{3}{4}$ feet off a 20-foot drain pipe. He then cut the remaining long piece into 5 pieces of equal length. Assuming no waste, what length in feet is each of the five equal pieces?

(1) $3\frac{1}{4}$

(4) $3\frac{3}{4}$

(2) $3\frac{3}{8}$

(5) Not enough information is given.

(3) $3\frac{1}{2}$

8. For $64 plus a small delivery charge, Bryce bought a truckload of $12\frac{1}{2}$ cubic yards of topsoil. At this price, what did Bryce pay to the nearest penny for each cubic yard of soil delivered to his home?

(1) $5.04

(4) $5.26

(2) $5.12

(5) Not enough information is given.

(3) $5.18

9. Grapes, normally selling in January at $1.69 per pound, are on sale for $1.49 per pound. During the sale, what will $3\frac{1}{4}$ pounds of grapes cost to the nearest cent?

(1) $4.72   (2) $4.84   (3) $4.98   (4) $5.06   (5) $5.18

10. Tony bought $4\frac{2}{3}$ pounds of hamburger to make a meatloaf. After cooking, the meatloaf's weight was down to $4\frac{1}{8}$ pounds. To divide the meatloaf into six equal pieces, what weight in pounds should Tony make each piece?

(1) $\frac{9}{16}$

(4) $\frac{9}{7}$

(2) $\frac{11}{16}$

(5) Not enough information is given.

(3) $\frac{7}{9}$

11. After he works 40 hours during the week, Phil is paid $1\frac{1}{2}$ times his normal hourly wage for any additional hours. Phil's average weekly overtime paycheck is for $45.60. How much overtime pay does Phil earn in a week in which he works $47\frac{1}{2}$ hours?

(1) $62.80

(4) $70.20

(2) $65.30

(5) Not enough information is given.

(3) $68.40

12. According to the map below, what fraction of the distance between Lee's house and the library is the distance between Lee's house and the public pool?

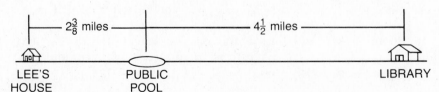

|— $2\frac{3}{8}$ miles —| |—————— $4\frac{1}{2}$ miles ——————|

LEE'S   PUBLIC   LIBRARY
HOUSE   POOL

ANSWERS ARE ON PAGE 96.

GED Practice
PART THREE

1. For the weekend barbecue, Grace has prepared $8\frac{1}{4}$ pounds of potato salad, $6\frac{1}{4}$ pounds of cole slaw, and $3\frac{5}{8}$ pounds of lettuce salad. If each person eats an average of $\frac{5}{8}$ pound of salad during the day-long picnic, how many people will this much salad feed?

   (1) 23   **(2)** 26   **(3)** 29   **(4)** 32   **(5)** 35

2. The results of 4 months of Bea's diet are shown at right. If she continues her diet and follows the same pattern of weight loss, how many more pounds will Bea lose during the next three months?

   (1) $12\frac{5}{8}$

   (2) $13\frac{3}{8}$

   (3) $14\frac{3}{4}$

   (4) $15\frac{3}{8}$

   (5) $16\frac{1}{8}$

Date	Bea's Weight
Feb. 1	180
March 1	$174\frac{5}{8}$
April 1	$169\frac{1}{4}$
May 1	$163\frac{7}{8}$
June 1	$158\frac{1}{2}$

Questions 3–6 refer to the following information.

On the weekend weather report, the meteorologist reported the following rainfall amounts for the first five days of October.

Monday	$\frac{5}{16}$ inch
Tuesday	$\frac{3}{8}$ inch
Wednesday	$\frac{5}{8}$ inch
Thursday	$1\frac{3}{16}$ inches
Friday	$1\frac{1}{4}$ inches

3. How much more rain fell on Thursday than fell on Wednesday?

   (1) $\frac{3}{8}$ inch   **(2)** $\frac{9}{16}$ inch   **(3)** $\frac{5}{8}$ inch   **(4)** $\frac{11}{16}$ inch   **(5)** $\frac{7}{8}$ inch

4. If the rainfall reported for Thursday is just $\frac{3}{32}$ inch less than the greatest amount ever recorded on the first Thursday in October, what is the record amount for this day?

   (1) $1\frac{3}{32}$ inches

   (2) $1\frac{9}{32}$ inches

   (3) $1\frac{3}{8}$ inches

   (4) $1\frac{1}{2}$ inches

   (5) $1\frac{5}{8}$ inches

5. How many total inches of rain fell during the 5 days reported?

   (1) $3\frac{3}{16}$ **(2)** $3\frac{1}{4}$ **(3)** $3\frac{11}{16}$ **(4)** $3\frac{3}{4}$ **(5)** $3\frac{7}{8}$

6. What is the average of the rainfall amounts reported for the five days?

   (1) $\frac{3}{8}$ inch   **(2)** $\frac{1}{2}$ inch   **(3)** $\frac{3}{4}$ inch   **(4)** $\frac{7}{8}$ inch   **(5)** $\frac{15}{16}$ inch

ANSWERS ARE ON PAGE 96.

7. Wei-Chuan bought a $2\frac{1}{2}$-pound package of chicken breasts on sale for $1.09 per pound and $3\frac{1}{4}$ pounds of cheese for $2.84 per pound. Which expression represents the total Wei-Chuan paid for these items?

   (1) $(\frac{5}{2} + 1.09) + (\frac{13}{4} + 2.84)$

   (2) $(\frac{5}{2} + \frac{13}{4}) + (1.09 + 2.84)$

   (3) $(\frac{5}{2} + \frac{13}{4})(1.09 + 2.84)$

   (4) $(\frac{5}{2})(2.84) + (\frac{13}{4})(1.09)$

   (5) $(\frac{5}{2})(1.09) + (\frac{13}{4})(2.84)$

Questions 8–11 refer to the following information.

Part of Lyle's job at the Buyer's Variety Store is to place price tags on sale items. During the 4th of July sale, Lyle was told to mark sale items as follows: Place tags reading "$\frac{1}{3}$ OFF" on all sale items of clothing, tags reading "$\frac{1}{2}$ OFF" on all sale hardware items, and tags reading "$\frac{1}{4}$ OFF" on all sale kitchen and dining items.

8. Expressed as a fraction of selling price, by how much more are the prices of sale hardware items being lowered than the prices of sale clothing items?

   (1) $\frac{1}{6}$ **(2)** $\frac{1}{5}$ **(3)** $\frac{1}{4}$ **(4)** $\frac{1}{3}$ **(5)** $\frac{1}{2}$

9. On which of the following sale items will a customer save the most money?

   (1) a hammer originally selling for $12.50
   (2) an electric frying pan originally selling for $22.88
   (3) a pair of pants originally selling for $18.99
   (4) a hand saw originally selling for $13.48
   (5) a skirt originally selling for $19.59

10. Expressed as a fraction, what is the average markdown Buyer's Variety Store is offering over the 4th of July weekend?

   (1) $\frac{5}{9}$ **(2)** $\frac{11}{18}$ **(3)** $\frac{13}{36}$ **(4)** $\frac{25}{36}$ **(5)** $\frac{3}{4}$

11. At the sale, Flo bought a shovel regularly selling for $18 and a blouse regularly selling for $23. If she paid with a $50 bill, which expression represents the amount of change she should receive?

   (1) $(\frac{1}{2})(18) + (\frac{2}{3})(23) - 50$

   (2) $(\frac{1}{2})(18) + (\frac{1}{3})(23) - 50$

   (3) $50 - (\frac{1}{2})(18) - (\frac{1}{3})(23)$

   (4) $50 - (\frac{1}{2})(18) - (\frac{2}{3})(23)$

   (5) $50 + (\frac{1}{2})(18) + (\frac{1}{3})(23)$

12. Gravel at Apex Sand and Gravel is sold according to weight. Four truckloads of different gravel size were weighed as shown below.

   Which of the following sequences represents the gravel from most expensive (heaviest) to least expensive (lightest)?

   (1) C, A, B, D
   (2) A, C, B, D
   (3) B, A, C, D
   (4) D, C, B, A
   (5) C, B, A, D

Type	Weight
Gravel A	1.6 tons
Gravel B	1.59 tons
Gravel C	$1\frac{5}{8}$ tons
Gravel D	$1\frac{9}{16}$ tons

ANSWERS ARE ON PAGE 96.

Questions 13–16 refer to the W-2 form shown below.

1 Control number 0046374		OMB No. 093862-1		
2 Employer's name, address, and ZIP code		3 Employer's identification number		4 Employer's state I.D. number
HOWARD MANUFACTURING COMPANY 5460 EAST RIVER STREET BEND, OREGON 97505		5 Statutory employee ☐ / Deceased ☐ / Pension plan ☐ / Legal rep. ☐	942 emp. ☐ / Subtotal ☐ / Deferred compensation ☐	Void ☐
		6 Allocated tips	7 Advance EIC payment	.00
8 Employee's social security number 453-84-7062	9 Federal income tax withheld $2,250.00	10 Wages, tips, other compensation $15,000.00	11 Social security tax withheld $990.00	
12 Employee's name, address, and ZIP code		13 Social security wages $15,000.00	14 Social security tips	
Kenneth Johnson 235 Highway West Bend, Oregon 97501		16	16a Fringe benefits incl. in Box 10	
		17 State income tax $740.00	18 State wages, tips, etc. $15,000.00	19 Name of state OR
		20 Local income tax	21 Local wages, tips, etc.	22 Name of locality

Form **W-2 Wage and Tax Statement** **1993**
Employee's and employer's copy compared ☐

Copy 1 For State, City, or Local Tax Department

13. What fraction of Kenneth's gross pay (identified as item 10, "Wages, tips, other compensation") did his employer withhold for federal taxes?

  (1) $\frac{1}{10}$ **(2)** $\frac{3}{20}$ **(3)** $\frac{4}{25}$ **(4)** $\frac{1}{6}$ **(5)** $\frac{4}{15}$

14. Approximately what fraction of Kenneth's gross pay did his employer withhold for social security?

  (1) $\frac{1}{15}$ **(2)** $\frac{1}{12}$ **(3)** $\frac{1}{10}$ **(4)** $\frac{1}{8}$ **(5)** $\frac{1}{6}$

15. Approximately what fraction of the amount withheld for federal taxes is the amount withheld for state taxes?

  (1) $\frac{1}{15}$ **(2)** $\frac{1}{10}$ **(3)** $\frac{1}{5}$ **(4)** $\frac{1}{4}$ **(5)** $\frac{1}{3}$

16. If Kenneth's income next year goes up by $\frac{1}{3}$ and the amount withheld also increases by $\frac{1}{3}$, what amount will Kenneth's employer deduct next year for federal taxes?

  (1) $1000   **(2)** $2000   **(3)** $3000   **(4)** $4000   **(5)** $5000

ANSWERS ARE ON PAGE 96.

Probability, Ratio, and Proportion

PART ONE

Questions 1–3 refer to the following spinner. Assume the spinner can't stop on a line.

1. What is the probability that the spinner will stop on $100?

2. What is the probability that the spinner will stop on a dollar amount less than $25?

3. What is the probability that the spinner will stop on a dollar amount greater than $25?

Directions: Find the following probabilities or ratios and reduce to lowest terms.

4. In Joe's drawer are 6 white undershirts and 4 light blue ones. If, in the dark, Joe reaches into his drawer and takes out an undershirt, what is the probability it will be blue?

5. Corey has 4 nickels, 2 dimes, and 3 pennies in his pocket. If he reaches in and pulls out the first coin he touches, what is the probability that Corey will choose a penny?

6. Lucy's package of taffy contains 4 raspberry, 3 chocolate, 5 cherry, and 2 lemon taffy chews. If Lucy reaches in and randomly takes out a piece of taffy, what is the probability she will pick a chocolate chew?

7. At a bingo game, Pamela has 4 of the 140 cards being played. What is the probability that Pamela will be the first to complete a row and win?

8. Fran's recipe calls for 3 cups of white flour for each 2 cups of whole-wheat flour. In this recipe, what is the ratio of whole-wheat flour to white flour?

9. In Gretchen's third-grade class are 14 girls and 12 boys. Determine the ratio of girls to boys in this class.

10. When he remodeled his house, John spent $2400 for materials and $4200 for labor. Find the ratio of the labor costs to the cost of materials.

11. Three of Evelyn's children are girls, and two are boys. What is the ratio of boy children to girl children in Evelyn's family?

12. For every $5 Laura earns, her husband, Stuart, earns $3.75. What is the ratio of Stuart's earnings to Laura's?

ANSWERS ARE ON PAGE 97.

Directions: In problems 13–15, find the missing term in each proportion.

13. $\frac{8}{p} = \frac{3}{9}$ **14.** $\frac{15}{40} = \frac{r}{8}$ **15.** $3{:}4 = n{:}64$

ANSWERS FOR PART ONE ARE ON PAGE 97.

PART TWO

1. If you randomly pick a number from 1 to 20, what is the probability that the number you pick will be evenly divisible by 5?

2. Three times each week, Walt takes a meat sandwich to work for lunch. The other two days, he takes a cheese sandwich. Today, just for fun, he and his buddy Duane traded lunch pails without telling each other what was in them. What is the probability that Duane ended up with a meat sandwich?

3. In a multiple-choice math test, Erin came to a problem she was unable to solve. However, she was certain that two of the five answer choices were not correct. If she was right about those two choices, what is the probability that Erin could guess the correct answer from the remaining choices?

4. In the middle of the night in a dark kitchen, Ken discovers that the refrigerator light is out. If 2 cartons of nonfat milk and 3 cartons of whole milk are inside, what is the probability that Ken can, with one try, grab a carton of the nonfat milk?

5. Seven buses leave the Market Street stop each hour, but only two of them go to Orchard Park. Michelle is unfamiliar with the bus routes and thinks that all seven go to Orchard Park. If she gets on a bus at Market Street, what is the probability that the bus will *not* go to Orchard Park?

6. Out of every 3000 radios that the Good Sound Company sells, 14 are defective. What is the probability that Anthony's new Good Sound radio is *not* defective?

7. Julia sent two dozen cookies to school with her daughter for the Valentine's Day party. Fourteen of the cookies were oatmeal, and the rest were chocolate chip. What is the ratio of chocolate chip cookies to oatmeal cookies?

8. Out of each 10 questions on the GED Mathematics Test, 5 are from the study of arithmetic questions, 3 from the study of algebra, and 2 from the study of geometry. On this test, what is the ratio of questions from the study of arithmetic to questions from studies other than arithmetic?

9. Three-eighths of the students in Grant's swimming class are men. What is the ratio of women to men in Grant's class?

   (1) $\frac{8}{11}$ **(2)** $\frac{11}{8}$ **(3)** $\frac{8}{3}$ **(4)** $\frac{5}{3}$ **(5)** $\frac{8}{5}$

10. From Buel's monthly gross pay of $1,600, her employer withholds $480. Of this $480, $100 goes into a company savings plan. What is the ratio of the amount Buel takes home each month to the amount that is withheld?

    (1) $\frac{17}{8}$ **(2)** $\frac{5}{4}$ **(3)** $\frac{9}{5}$ **(4)** $\frac{7}{3}$ **(5)** $\frac{11}{6}$

11. In Clem's hometown, 2 out of every 5 adults do not have a high school diploma. However, 1 adult in 10 without a diploma is enrolled in a GED program. In this town, what is the ratio of the number of adults with a high school diploma to those without one?

    (1) $\frac{3}{10}$ **(2)** $\frac{3}{2}$ **(3)** $\frac{3}{5}$ **(4)** $\frac{1}{2}$ **(5)** $\frac{7}{10}$

ANSWERS ARE ON PAGE 97.

12. Of the 31 days in March, rain fell on 12 days, snow fell on 6 days, and the remaining days were clear. During this month, what was the ratio of the days on which rain didn't fall to the days on which it did?

(1) $\frac{1}{2}$ **(2)** $\frac{12}{31}$ **(3)** $\frac{19}{12}$ **(4)** $\frac{19}{31}$ **(5)** $\frac{19}{18}$

13. In a well-balanced 2500-calorie diet, 1500 calories are obtained from carbohydrates, while no more than 750 calories come from fat. The remaining calories come from protein. In a well-balanced diet, what is the ratio of the calories obtained from protein to the calories obtained from carbohydrates?

(1) $\frac{1}{5}$ **(2)** $\frac{1}{6}$ **(3)** $\frac{1}{7}$ **(4)** $\frac{1}{8}$ **(5)** $\frac{1}{9}$

ANSWERS FOR PART TWO ARE ON PAGE 97.

═ GED Practice ═
PART THREE

Questions 1–2 refer to the following drawing.

1. Suppose the 5 cards shown above are placed upside down and mixed up. What is the probability of picking a face card at random on your first try?

(1) $\frac{2}{3}$ **(2)** $\frac{5}{2}$ **(3)** $\frac{3}{5}$ **(4)** $\frac{2}{5}$ **(5)** $\frac{3}{2}$

2. If on your first try you pick a face card and don't put it back, what is the probability of picking another face card on your second try?

(1) $\frac{1}{3}$ **(2)** $\frac{1}{2}$ **(3)** $\frac{2}{3}$ **(4)** $\frac{3}{4}$ **(5)** $\frac{4}{5}$

Questions 3–6 refer to the following information.

Take-Home Taco sells four kinds of tacos. Out of each 10 tacos they sell, 3 are Plain Tacos selling for $1.00 each, 4 are Super Tacos selling for $1.30 each, 2 are Tacos Grandes selling for $1.60 each, and 1 is a Pizza Taco selling for $2.00.

3. What is the ratio of the number of Super Tacos sold to the number of Plain Tacos sold?

(1) $\frac{1}{4}$ **(2)** $\frac{3}{4}$ **(3)** $\frac{4}{3}$ **(4)** $\frac{5}{4}$ **(5)** $\frac{4}{7}$

4. What is the probability that a customer who orders a taco will order a Taco Grande?

(1) $\frac{1}{5}$ **(2)** $\frac{1}{4}$ **(3)** $\frac{1}{3}$ **(4)** $\frac{1}{7}$ **(5)** $\frac{2}{7}$

5. What is the ratio of the amount of money brought in from the sale of Tacos Grandes to the amount brought in from the sale of Super Tacos?

(1) $\frac{4}{7}$ **(2)** $\frac{5}{9}$ **(3)** $\frac{7}{11}$ **(4)** $\frac{8}{13}$ **(5)** $\frac{9}{15}$

ANSWERS ARE ON PAGE 97.

6. What is the ratio of the number of Plain Tacos sold to the number of tacos sold that are not Plain Tacos?

    (1) $\frac{3}{7}$ **(2)** $\frac{3}{10}$ **(3)** $\frac{3}{4}$ **(4)** $\frac{3}{13}$ **(5)** $\frac{3}{5}$

7. The scale on a county map says that $\frac{1}{2}$ inch of map distance is equal to 4 miles of actual distance. If two points are $2\frac{1}{2}$ inches apart on the map, how many miles apart are they in actual distance?

    (1) $2\frac{1}{2}$ **(2)** 5   **(3)** $7\frac{1}{2}$ **(4)** 10   **(5)** 20

8. Best Buy Market is selling lettuce at 3 heads for $1.44. At this rate, how much do 8 heads of lettuce cost?

    (1) $3.84   **(2)** $5.24   **(3)** $6.08   **(4)** $7.62   **(5)** $11.52

9. At Adam's Bakery, chocolate chip cookies are selling for $1.92 per dozen. At this rate, what does Adam charge for 7 cookies?

    (1) $.88   **(2)** $1.06   **(3)** $1.12   **(4)** $1.24   **(5)** $1.36

10. Roger purchased a print of a famous painting. The actual painting is 8 feet long and 6 feet wide. If the length of the print is 20 inches, which of the following expressions represents the width of the print?

    (1) $(\frac{6}{8})(20)$ **(4)** $(6 + 8)(20)$

    (2) $(\frac{8}{6})(20)$ **(5)** $20 - 8$

    (3) $\frac{(8)(20)}{6}$

11. It takes Francis 50 minutes to walk 3 miles. Which expression represents the length of time in minutes it would take Francis to walk 7 miles if he walked at the same rate?

    (1) $7(50 - 3)$ **(2)** $\frac{(3)(50)}{7}$ **(3)** $\frac{(7)(3)}{50}$ **(4)** $7\frac{50}{3}$ **(5)** $\frac{50}{(7)(3)}$

12. Kristal's bowling team won 4 league games for every 3 games they lost. If they played in 28 games before the start of the summer tournament, how many games had they won up to this point?

    (1) 10   **(2)** 12   **(3)** 14   **(4)** 16   **(5)** 18

13. For every 8 people who order hamburgers at Michael's Burgers, 2 other people order chili. During a day when 260 customers order hamburgers, how many orders of chili can Michael expect to sell?

    (1) 35   **(2)** 50   **(3)** 65   **(4)** 80   **(5)** 95

14. Out of every dollar he makes, Mark puts $.04 in a savings account and invests $.06 in the stock market. If he put a total of $900 in these two types of investments last year, how much did he put in his savings account?

    (1) $360   **(2)** $400   **(3)** $440   **(4)** $480   **(5)** $520

15. For every two American-made cars he sells off his used-car lot, Brent usually sells three foreign-made cars. If this pattern holds during a month when he sells 55 cars, how many of them will be foreign-made?

    (1) 28   **(2)** 30   **(3)** 33   **(4)** 37   **(5)** 44

ANSWERS ARE ON PAGE 97.

16. Shown on his drawing at right, Cal measured the shadows of two skyscrapers that stand across the street from Central Park. Knowing the number of stories of the shorter building, which expression below tells him the approximate number of stories of the taller buildings?

(1) $\frac{325 - 200}{48}$

(2) $(48)(325 + 200)$

(3) $(48)(325 - 200)$

(4) $(\frac{48}{325})200$

(5) $(\frac{48}{200})325$

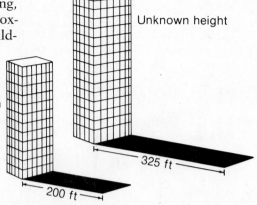

Unknown height

48 stories high

325 ft

200 ft

17. A shortwave radio antenna is attached to the roof of Jill's house by support cables. As shown in the drawing at right, the upper and lower cables are parallel and attach to the flat roof at equal angles. If the lower cable is 9 feet long, which of the following expressions represents the length of the upper cable?

(1) $(\frac{4}{9})(7)$

(2) $(\frac{9}{4})(7)$

(3) $\frac{9}{(7)(4)}$

(4) $(9)(4)(7)$

(5) $\frac{(7)(4)}{9}$

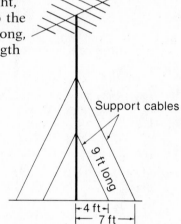

Support cables

9 ft long

4 ft

7 ft

ANSWERS ARE ON PAGE 98.

Percents

Text pages 131–163

PART ONE

1. What is 8% of 400?

2. Eighteen is what percent of 9?

3. Forty-two is forty percent of what number?

4. 85% of what number equals 17?

5. What is 26% of 850?

6. 7 is what percent of 50?

7. Before Sunday's sale, a dining set Connie liked was selling for $950. On Sunday, the price was reduced by 20%. Find the dollar amount of this price reduction.

8. During a year when the inflation rate is 5%, how much can you expect the cost of $150 worth of groceries—at today's prices—to increase in cost in 1 year's time?

9. Part of Jean's New Year's resolution is to save 10% of her monthly take-home income. How much does Jean plan to save each month out of the $845 she brings home?

10. When he bought his $106,000 house, Luke had to make a down payment of $7420. Express Luke's down payment as a percent of the sales price.

11. During the year, the average price of a $12,000 new car increased by $360. What percent inflation rate does this price increase represent?

12. When he passed his GED math test, Danny got 38 out of 56 questions correct. To the nearest percent, what percent of the questions did Danny answer correctly?

13. Joel's employer withholds $3072 of Joel's gross yearly salary of $19,200. What percent of Joel's income is withheld?

14. Twenty-five percent of Khalid's monthly salary goes to pay for rent. If his rent is $326 per month, how much does Khalid earn each month?

15. During the last presidential election, 26% of the registered Republicans in Lynn County voted. If 7358 Republicans voted, how many registered voters in Lynn County are Republicans?

16. Vivian bought a table on sale for $288. If the table was sold for 80% of its regular price, what was its price before the sale?

17. Over the holiday weekend, Leland Motors sold 15% of the pickups it had on its lot. If 9 pickups were sold that weekend, how many were on the lot before the sale?

ANSWERS ARE ON PAGE 98.

PART TWO

1. A sweater that regularly sells for $39.00 is marked down 30% during a weekend sale. Find the sale price of this sweater.

2. Paying a state sales tax of 5%, how much will Daryl actually pay for a washing machine that's on sale for $289.00?

3. Because of a business slowdown, Hollie is asked to agree to a 7% pay cut. If her income before the proposed cut is $14,000 per year, what would her income become if she agrees to the decrease?

4. When the speed limit was reduced from 65 to 55 miles per hour, traffic fatalities in Bentley County decreased by 30%. If, before the speed decrease, the county averaged 20 traffic deaths per year, how many does the county average now?

5. Benson received a property tax bill for $684 in early November. If he pays the total bill before the end of December, he will be given a 3% discount. If Benson pays the total on December 15, for how much should he write the check?

6. At Auto Specialty Shop, Greg adds a 25% markup to each item he sells. What is Greg's selling price of a gasket he buys from the wholesaler for $2.36?

7. During the first year he owned his new car, the value of Ted's car depreciated (decreased) 22%. If the car cost $10,400 new, what was its value at the end of the first year?

8. The first year Sarah owned her house, its value rose from $92,000 to $95,680. What percent increase does this gain in value represent?

9. Two years after Eiko Auto Electric bought an engine analyzer for $4840, its value had decreased to $2662. What percent decrease in value does this represent?

10. Because of competition from other restaurants, Hamburger Champ lowered the price of its Champ Burger from $2.80 to $2.38. By what percent was the price of the Champ Burger reduced?

11. When he began his diet, Lloyd weighed 200 pounds. During the next 6 months, he lost 34 pounds. Determine the percent of body weight that Lloyd lost.

12. When they raised the price of the large popcorn from $1.50 to $2.00, Cinema Plus found that average daily popcorn sales decreased from 360 to 270. By what percent did the number of sales decline?

   (1) 20%   **(2)** 25%   **(3)** 30%   **(4)** $33\frac{1}{3}$%   **(5)** 50%

13. Because of an 8.9% rise in the cost of vegetables during winter, the price of the salad bar at Food Delight increased from $2.48 to $2.74. To the nearest percent, by what percent did Food Delight raise the price of its salad bar?

   (1) 9%   **(2)** 10%   **(3)** 12%   **(4)** 13%   **(5)** 16%

14. On an unpaid balance of $240 on his Visa card, Vance was charged $43.20 during July, bringing his new balance to $283.20. Determine the monthly interest rate of Vance's Visa card.

   (1) 11%   **(2)** 13%   **(3)** 15%   **(4)** 18%   **(5)** 21%

ANSWERS ARE ON PAGE 98.

15. Penny found a jacket that was comparable to others selling for $49. This jacket was marked "20% off," and Penny paid only $34 for it. If the jacket hadn't been on sale, what price would Penny have had to pay?

16. The 18 members of Thelma's aerobics class represent only 40 percent of the membership of the class one year ago. How many people quit coming to the class during the last year?

17. Because he paid cash, Gary received a 6% discount when he bought his stereo. If he paid $446.50 for the stereo, how much would he have paid without the discount?

18. What total amount will Barry have to repay his credit union after 1 year 9 months for a loan of $500 borrowed at 16% simple interest?

19. Kellie borrowed $2000 from her credit union to help pay for a used car. If the credit union charged her an interest rate of 14%, what total amount would be due at the end of one year, when Kellie plans to pay back the loan?

20. If Kyle deposits $1500, how much interest can Kyle earn in 6 months' time in a savings account that pays $3\frac{1}{2}\%$ interest?

    (1) $22.50 **(2)** $26.25 **(3)** $45.00 **(4)** $52.50 **(5)** $105.00

ANSWERS FOR PART TWO BEGIN ON PAGE 98.

GED Practice
PART THREE

1. If Tim borrows $2500 at 20% simple interest for 9 months, what total amount will be due at the end of that period?

   (1) $2123 **(2)** $2520 **(3)** $2875 **(4)** $3125 **(5)** $3350

2. A month before Christmas, Toy Palace reduced the price of all toys by 20%. During the week of Christmas, they reduced the sale price itself by 20% for all toys over $25. On December 23, how much would Blanche have to pay for a doll set that originally sold for $36?

   (1) $20.00   **(4)** $23.80
   (2) $22.17   **(5)** Not enough information is given.
   (3) $23.04

3. In the November special election, 64 percent of the registered voters of the county voted. Fifty-five percent of those who voted were Democrats. If 28,500 of the 53,400 county residents are registered voters, how many Democrats voted?

   (1) 8940   **(4)** 13,080
   (2) 10,032   **(5)** Not enough information is given.
   (3) 12,138

4. During an 8:00-to-Midnight Sale, customers at Helga's Furniture can take an additional 10% off the price of any item in the store, even those already marked down. What will a customer pay for a lamp originally priced at $120 and marked on sale for $33\frac{1}{3}\%$ off?

   (1) $62 **(2)** $65 **(3)** $67 **(4)** $69 **(5)** $72

ANSWERS ARE ON PAGE 98.

5. Two hundred forty tickets were sold for the school picnic, but 25% of the ticket holders did not show up. Of those who came, 65% were women. What percent of those who did not show up were men?

(1) 35   (4) 75
(2) 60   (5) Not enough information is given.
(3) 68

6. If you borrowed $1500 for one year at an interest rate of 21%, how much more would you have to pay than if the interest rate were 10%?

(1) $105   (2) $125   (3) $145   (4) $165   (5) $185

7. Jason has completed 19 miles of a 75-mile bike race. Which expression gives the fraction of the race he has not yet completed?

(1) $\frac{19}{75}$ (2) $\frac{75}{19}$ (3) $\frac{75-19}{19}$ (4) $\frac{75-19}{75}$ (5) $\frac{75-19}{75+19}$

8. Twelve teams signed up for the bowling tournament over the weekend. If 85% of the teams signed in by 9:00 A.M. Saturday, which expression gives the number of teams that had *not* signed in by that time?

(1) (.85)(12)   (4) (12 − 1)(.85)
(2) (1 − .85)(12)   (5) (.12)(85)
(3) (1 + .85)(12)

9. Before he received an 8% raise, Manuel's monthly salary was $1250. Which expression gives Manuel's monthly salary after he got the raise?

(1) (.08)($1250)   (4) (.92)($1250)
(2) $1250 + (.08)($1250)   (5) (.92)($1250) + $1250
(3) $1250 − (.08)($1250)

10. To buy new carpet, Jennie needs to borrow $2000 for 1 year. She contacted 5 loan companies, and was offered the terms listed below. Under which of the following conditions would Jennie pay the least total interest?

(1) make 12 payments of $185, one at the end of each month
(2) make 3 payments of $741, one at the end of each 4 months
(3) make 4 payments of $564, one at the end of each 3 months
(4) pay back a total of $2345 at the end of the year
(5) pay back $2000 plus 18% interest at the end of the year

Questions 11–13 refer to the following situation.

> During an after-Easter sale, Ben's Recreation Center and Value Hardware each offered special buys on a gas barbecue that Chris wanted to buy and have delivered as an assembled unit. Ben's discounted the $189 barbecue by 15%, offered Chris a $10 factory rebate (available only at Ben's), and promised to assemble the barbecue for free and to deliver it for $5. Value Hardware agreed to reduce their $192 selling price by $24, to reduce the $15 assembly charge, and to provide delivery for $3—a $7 savings.

11. Considering the rebate, what would be Chris's total cost to purchase the assembled, delivered barbecue from Ben's?

(1) $132.85   (4) $161.25
(2) $148.95   (5) Not enough information is given.
(3) $155.65

ANSWERS ARE ON PAGE 99.

12. By what percent is Value Hardware decreasing the retail selling price of the barbecue?

    (1) $12\frac{1}{2}\%$

    (2) $16\frac{2}{3}\%$

    (3) 25%

    (4) $33\frac{1}{3}\%$

    (5) Not enough information is given.

13. What additional information does Chris need to know to determine which of the two stores is offering the better buy?

    (1) the price for which someone else would do the assembly
    (2) the usual assembly price at each store
    (3) the amount Value Hardware will charge for assembly
    (4) the length of time for which the $10 rebate is good
    (5) the usual delivery price at each store

Questions 14–16 refer to the following situation.

> Debbie Manskey plans to purchase a used car. One possibility is a three-year-old Honda selling for $6200. The salesman will discount the selling price 12% if Debbie pays cash, and he will give her $2700 for her trade-in. The second car Debbie is considering is a two-year-old Chevrolet on sale at a lot across the state line for $5700. Although no sales tax is required on the Honda, a 4% sales tax would be charged on the Chevrolet. The Chevrolet salesman will give Debbie 30% more for her trade-in than the Honda salesman, and he will also give a discount for cash.

14. If she trades in her old car, how much cash would Debbie need to purchase the Honda?

    (1) $2184
    (2) $2756
    (3) $3465

    (4) $3980
    (5) Not enough information is given.

15. What amount is the Chevrolet salesman offering Debbie for her trade-in?

    (1) $2730
    (2) $3000
    (3) $3145

    (4) $3510
    (5) Not enough information is given.

16. If she trades in her old car and pays cash, what amount would Debbie need to purchase the Chevrolet?

    (1) $1707
    (2) $2143
    (3) $2418

    (4) $2984
    (5) Not enough information is given.

ANSWERS ARE ON PAGE 99.

Measurement

PART ONE

Directions: Complete each measurement chart below.

Measures of Length

1. 1 foot = _____ inches
2. 1 yard = _____ feet
3. 1 yard = _____ inches
4. 1 mile = _____ feet
5. 1 mile = _____ yards
6. 1 meter = _____ millimeters
7. 1 meter = _____ centimeters
8. 1 kilometer = _____ meters

Liquid Measures

9. 1 pint = _____ ounces
10. 1 cup = _____ ounces
11. 1 pint = _____ cups
12. 1 quart = _____ pints
13. 1 gallon = _____ quarts
14. 1 liter = _____ milliliters
15. 1 liter = _____ centiliters
16. 1 liter = _____ deciliters

Measures of Time

17. 1 minute = _____ seconds
18. 1 hour = _____ minutes
19. 1 day = _____ hours
20. 1 week = _____ days
21. 1 year = _____ days

Measures of Weight

22. 1 pound = _____ ounces
23. 1 ton = _____ pounds
24. 1 gram = _____ milligrams
25. 1 gram = _____ centigrams
26. 1 kilogram = _____ grams

27. On her eighth birthday, Brenda measured 48 inches tall. How many feet tall was Brenda when she turned eight?

28. During the coming weekend, Millie plans to can $4\frac{1}{2}$ gallons of cooked beans in quart jars. How many jars will Millie need?

29. The top of Mount McKinley, the highest mountain in North America, is 20,320 feet above sea level. To the nearest mile, what is the height of this mountain?

30. Julia's favorite recipe for sparkling punch calls for $2\frac{1}{2}$ cups of 7-Up to be mixed with each quart of fruit juice. For each quart of fruit juice she uses in the punch, how many ounces of 7-Up should Julia add?

31. During the Fourth of July weekend, Jose was on call day and night as a Forest Service fire fighter. How many hours was Jose on call during this four-day holiday period?

32. For use in her garden, Jeanne purchased a 25-yard-long hose. What is the length of this hose in feet?

40

ANSWERS ARE ON PAGE 99.

33. How many ounces of chicken are contained in a 3-pound package of boned chicken meat?

34. Large soft drinks in foreign countries are sold in 500-milliliter cups. How many of these large cups can be filled from 1 liter of soft drink?

35. Erik bought a pair of skis that measured 200 centimeters long. Express this length in meters.

36. A piece of imported cheese was labeled as weighing 0.65 kg. What is the weight of this cheese in grams?

37. Terry's watch band is 12.4 centimeters long. What is the length of this band in millimeters?

38. An imported cough medicine comes in one-deciliter glass bottles. If a pharmacy orders 24.5 liters of this cough medicine, how many bottles can it expect to receive?

39. What is the approximate reading in amperes of the electric current indicated on the following meter dial?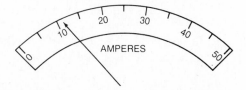

ANSWERS FOR PART ONE BEGIN ON PAGE 99.

PART TWO

1. A standard high school or college track is 440 yards around. How many laps does a runner complete when running in a 3-mile race?

2. Pat can haul 750 pounds of fill dirt in his pickup at one time. How many trips will Pat need to make in order to haul 5 tons of dirt?

3. Shown on the chart at the right is the amount of time Shannon read last week during after-school hours. What total amount of time in hours is listed on this chart?

Monday	48 minutes
Tuesday	93 minutes
Wednesday	20 minutes
Thursday	75 minutes
Friday	64 minutes

4. On Saturday, Kimberly worked 75 minutes of overtime. If she is paid $2.80 for each $\frac{1}{4}$ hour of overtime, how much did Kimberly earn in overtime Saturday?

5. If Stacey practices her guitar for 35 minutes each day, how much total time in hours and minutes does she practice in six days?

6. For dinner Friday evening, Sharon bought a large steak that she plans to cut into three equal pieces. If the uncut steak weighs 1 pound 14 ounces, what should be the weight of each cut piece?

7. By train, the trip between Oakville and Grass Valley takes 4 hours 12 minutes. One-third of the way to Grass Valley, the train stops in Harmon. If Jeff takes the 8:35 A.M. train out of Oakville, at what time will he arrive at Harmon?

ANSWERS ARE ON PAGE 99.

8. During a 100-mile bicycle race, Ralph stopped to fix a flat tire after having traveled 64 miles 490 yards. At this point, how far in miles and yards is Ralph from the finish line?

9. Monday morning, Clark mailed four packages, two weighing 3 pounds 11 ounces each and two weighing 4 pounds 7 ounces each. What total weight of packages did Clark mail that morning?

10. Because of a rush job, Janice worked 1 hour 40 minutes overtime on Friday, six and one-half hours overtime on Saturday, and 3.5 hours of overtime on Sunday. Expressed as hours and minutes, how much total overtime did Janice work these three days?

11. If 1.6 kilometers is equal to 1 mile, what is the speed limit in kilometers per hour on a highway where the speed limit is 55 miles per hour?

12. A metric cup holds 250 milliliters. How many metric cups are called for in a French recipe that requires $1\frac{1}{2}$ liters of milk?

13. As shown on the scales below, what is the difference in weight between the tomato and the piece of cheese?

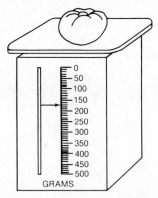 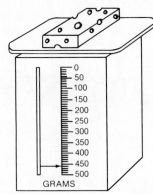

14. Len's weight before his diet is indicated on the scale below at the left. His weight after 3 months of dieting is indicated on the scale at the right. How much weight has Len lost?

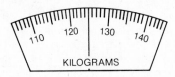 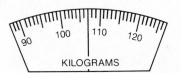

15. How much more liquid is contained in cup B below than in cup A?

A   B

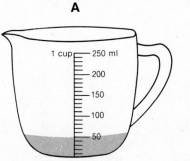 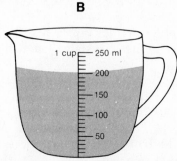

ANSWERS ARE ON PAGE 99.

GED Practice
PART THREE

1. How much higher than normal human body temperature is the temperature indicated on the clinical thermometer below?

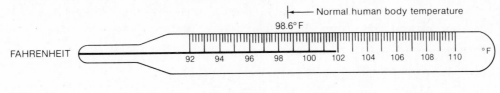

Normal human body temperature
98.6° F
FAHRENHEIT
92 94 96 98 100 102 104 106 108 110 °F

   (1) 2.2° F   **(2)** 2.6° F   **(3)** 3.0° F   **(4)** 3.2° F   **(5)** 3.6° F

2. Which of the following correctly represents the weight shown on the scale below?

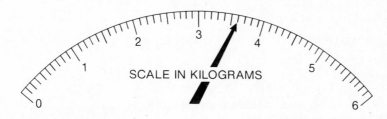

SCALE IN KILOGRAMS

   A. 3 kilograms 60 grams
   B. 3.6 kilograms
   C. 3 kilograms 600 grams
   D. 3.06 kilograms

   (1) A and B only   **(4)** B and C only
   (2) A and C only   **(5)** B and D only
   (3) A and D only

3. For Halloween treats, Mary bought 6 bags of candy, each weighing 1 pound 13 ounces. After mixing all the candy together, she will divide it into 30 small treat bags to give to children. To the nearest ounce, how much candy will each treat bag contain?

   (1) 4   **(2)** 5   **(3)** 6   **(4)** 7   **(5)** 8

4. Marquita, who lives in Miami, called her friend Therese in Chicago on Sunday morning. She waited until 11:00 A.M. (Miami time) to place the call because Miami is one hour later than Chicago. If they talked for 25 minutes, at what time (Chicago time) did Therese hang up the phone?

   (1) 9:35 A.M.   **(4)** 12:25 P.M.
   (2) 10:25 A.M.   **(5)** Not enough information is given.
   (3) 11:35 A.M.

5. Byron uses 1 pint of paint thinner for each three gallons of oil-based paint. During a year in which he painted 25 houses with oil-based paint, he averaged 6 gallons of paint per house. How much paint thinner did he use that year?

   (1) 5 gallons 1 quart   **(4)** 7 gallons 1 quart
   (2) 6 gallons exactly   **(5)** Not enough information is given.
   (3) 6 gallons 1 quart

ANSWERS ARE ON PAGE 100.

6. What is the reading on the following 3 dials of a meter? When an arrow is between two numbers, read the *smaller* of the two numbers.

(1) 41.7 cu ft
(2) 417 cu ft
(3) 4,170 cu ft
(4) 41,700 cu ft
(5) 417,000 cu ft

7. Stephen is to stack bins of nails according to weight, placing the heaviest bin on the bottom and lighter bins on top. The weights of the bins are written as follows:

Bin A: 8 pounds 8 ounces

Bin B: 130 ounces

Bin C: $8\frac{1}{4}$ pounds

Bin D: 109 ounces

Listing the heaviest bin first, which sequence correctly lists the order in which the bins should be stacked?

(1) A, B, C, D
(2) B, D, A, C
(3) C, A, D, B
(4) A, C, B, D
(5) B, D, A, C

8. As part of his job at a ski shop, Julius arranges skis in a display rack. He places the tallest skis at the left and the shortest skis at the right. Below are listed four sizes of skis he must now place in the rack.

A. 2 meters 15 centimeters
B. 2.09 meters
C. 195 centimeters
D. 2 meters 3 centimeters

Which of the following sequences lists the order from left to right that the skis should be placed in the display rack?

(1) D, A, C, B
(2) B, A, D, C
(3) A, B, D, C
(4) D, C, B, A
(5) A, D, C, B

9. On Saturday, Jan is flying from Seattle to New York City. She is leaving Seattle at 9:10 A.M. on a flight that takes 4 hours and 45 minutes. If New York time is three hours later than Seattle time, which expression below represents the New York time at which Jan will arrive?

(1) 9:10 A.M. − 3 hours − 4 hours 45 minutes
(2) 9:10 A.M. + 3 hours − 4 hours 45 minutes
(3) 9:10 A.M. − 3 hours + 4 hours 45 minutes
(4) 9:10 A.M. + 3 hours + 4 hours 45 minutes
(5) 9:10 A.M. + 7 hours − 45 minutes

10. For a stained-glass window, Lee needs to cut a 3-foot, 8-inch sheet of glass into several small lengths. First, she will cut off one 9-inch-long piece. Then, she will cut the remaining sheet into 7 pieces of equal length. Which expression below represents the length in inches of each shorter piece?

(1) $\frac{36 + 8 - 9}{7}$

(2) $\frac{36 - 8 - 9}{7}$

(3) $\frac{36 + 8 + 9}{7}$

(4) $(36 - 9)(7) - 8$

(5) $(36 - 8)(7) - 9$

ANSWERS ARE ON PAGE 100.

1 1. On his new diet, Miklos set a goal of losing 0.5 kilogram each week. Shown at right are the amounts he actually lost during the first four weeks. Which of the following represents in kilograms the total weight Miklos lost during the weeks shown?

	Weight Lost
1st Week	300 g
2nd Week	400 g
3rd Week	700 g
4th Week	600 g

- **(1)** (500 + 300 + 400 + 700 + 600)(1000)

- **(2)** (300 + 400 + 700 + 600 − 500)(1000)

- **(3)** $\frac{300 + 400 + 700 + 600 - 500}{1000}$

- **(4)** (300 + 400 + 700 + 600)(1000)

- **(5)** $\frac{300 + 400 + 700 + 600}{1000}$

12. Friendly Market advertises "lean hamburger—only 10% fat." How many ounces of fat are contained in each pound of Friendly's lean hamburger?

- **(1)** 0.8
- **(2)** 1.6
- **(3)** 2.1
- **(4)** 4.3
- **(5)** Not enough information is given.

13. Working a 40-hour week, approximately what percent of the total hours in a 7-day week does Tad work?

- **(1)** 12%　　**(2)** 17%　　**(3)** 24%　　**(4)** 29%　　**(5)** 35%

14. A metric tablespoon holds 15 milliliters. About how many metric tablespoons of oil are needed in a recipe that calls for 1 deciliter of vegetable oil?

- **(1)** between 2 and 3
- **(2)** between 3 and 4
- **(3)** between 4 and 5
- **(4)** between 5 and 6
- **(5)** between 6 and 7

15. For the weekend barbecue, Henry is expecting to feed 18 people. Assuming that each person will consume 11 ounces of hamburger, how much hamburger should Henry buy?

- **(1)** 12 lb 6 oz
- **(2)** 14 lb 10 oz
- **(3)** 15 lb 13 oz
- **(4)** 16 lb 9 oz
- **(5)** 17 lb 12 oz

16. Shown below are the dials of a power meter. What is the total number of kilowatt-hours indicated by these dials? If the arrow falls between two numbers, read the *smaller* of the two numbers.

10,000

1,000

100

10

1

KILOWATT-HOURS

- **(1)** 22,426　　**(2)** 29,325　　**(3)** 32,436　　**(4)** 39,547　　**(5)** 43,547

ANSWERS ARE ON PAGE 100.

Graphs and Tables

Questions 1–10 refer to the pictograph shown below.

AVERAGE YEARLY SALARIES OF SELECTED JOBS
IN CHAPMAN COUNTY

Doctor	$ ¢ ¢
Electronics repairman	$ $ $ $ $ ¢ ¢
Food services worker	$ $ $ ¢
Insurance agent	$ $ $ $ $ $ ¢ ¢
Lawyer	$ $ $ $ $ $ $ $ $ $ $ $ $ $ ¢ ¢
Plumber	$ $ $ $ $ $ ¢
Retail sales worker	$ $ $
Schoolteacher	$ $ $ $ $ $ ¢ ¢

KEY
$ = $5,000
¢ = $1,000

PART ONE

1. What is the ratio of the value of the $ symbol to the ¢ symbol?

2. In which profession shown is the average yearly salary the lowest?

3. Earning $20,800 as a used-car salesman, Phil Davis earns about the same salary as people employed in which listed profession?

PART TWO

4. The values presented on the graph are rounded off to which of the following amounts?

   (1) to the nearest $10
   (2) to the nearest $100
   (3) to the nearest $1000
   (4) to the nearest $10,000
   (5) to the nearest $100,000

5. By how much does the highest average yearly salary shown on the graph differ from the lowest average yearly salary shown?

ANSWERS ARE ON PAGE 101.

6. What is the approximate ratio of the salary of a food services worker to the salary of a lawyer?

   (1) $\frac{1}{5}$

   (2) $\frac{5}{13}$

   (3) $\frac{3}{8}$

   (4) $\frac{2}{3}$

   (5) $\frac{3}{4}$

7. Cecil Banks, owner of a clothing store in Chapman County, earned $35,000 last year. What percent of the average salary of a retail sales worker did he earn?

   (1) 30%
   (2) 57%
   (3) 84%
   (4) 100%
   (5) 175%

ANSWERS ARE ON PAGE 101.

GED Practice
PART THREE

8. In Chapman County, which job category has an average salary that is 30% lower than the average salary of school teachers?

   (1) food services worker
   (2) electronics repairman
   (3) retail sales worker
   (4) plumber
   (5) insurance agent

9. Which of the following expressions represents the average of the salaries earned by doctors and lawyers in Chapman County?

   (1) $(22\frac{2}{5} + 16\frac{2}{5})(5000)$

   (2) $\frac{1}{2}(22\frac{2}{5} + 16\frac{2}{5})(5000)$

   (3) $\frac{1}{2}(24 + 18)(1000)$

   (4) $\frac{1}{2}(22 + 2 + 16 + 2)(5000)$

   (5) Not enough information is given.

10. Which expression below represents the ratio of the number of plumbers in Chapman County to the number of insurance agents?

   (1) $\frac{7}{9}$

   (2) $\frac{9}{7}$

   (3) $\frac{19}{23}$

   (4) $\frac{23}{19}$

   (5) Not enough information is given.

ANSWERS ARE ON PAGE 101.

Questions 11–23 refer to the circle graphs below.

MONTHLY INCOME AND BUDGET OF TURNER FAMILY

TURNER MONTHLY INCOME
($4,800)

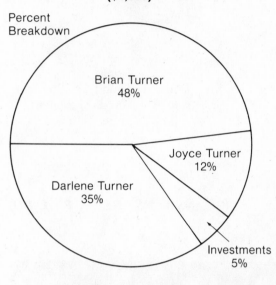

Percent
Breakdown

Brian Turner
48%

Joyce Turner
12%

Darlene Turner
35%

Investments
5%

TURNER MONTHLY BUDGET
($4,800)

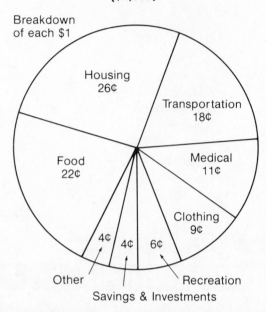

Breakdown
of each $1

Housing
26¢

Transportation
18¢

Food
22¢

Medical
11¢

Clothing
9¢

4¢   4¢   6¢

Other

Recreation

Savings & Investments

PART ONE

11. What percent of the family income is earned by Brian Turner?

12. What percent of the family income is earned together by Darlene and her daughter Joyce?

13. Out of each dollar of the Turner family income, how much is spent for housing?

14. Out of each dollar of the Turner family income, how much is spent on food and clothing expenses?

15. How much does Joyce Turner earn each month on her part-time job?

16. How much does the Turner family spend each month on medical expenses?

PART TWO

17. How much more does Brian earn each month than Darlene?

18. How much more do the Turners spend each month on housing costs than they spend on food?

19. What is the approximate ratio of what the Turners spend each month on housing to what they spend on clothing?

    (1) 2 to 1
    (2) 3 to 1
    (3) 4 to 1
    (4) 5 to 1
    (5) 6 to 1

ANSWERS ARE ON PAGE 101.

20. If Darlene receives a raise of $100 per month, by about what percent will the Turner family income increase?

(1) 1%

(2) 2%

(3) $3\frac{1}{2}$%

(4) 5%

(5) 6%

21. What is the average of the Turners' monthly payments for housing, transportation, and food?

(1) $840
(2) $1056
(3) $1092
(4) $1152
(5) Not enough information is given.

22. If Darlene quit her job, by what percent would the family expenses for transportation decrease?

(1) 9%
(2) 18%
(3) 27%
(4) 35%
(5) Not enough information is given.

23. If Brian lost his job but received $1200 per month in unemployment benefits, by about what percent would the Turner family income decrease?

(1) 48%
(2) 39%
(3) 20%
(4) 9%
(5) Not enough information is given.

ANSWERS ARE ON PAGE 101.

Questions 24–30 refer to the bar graph below.

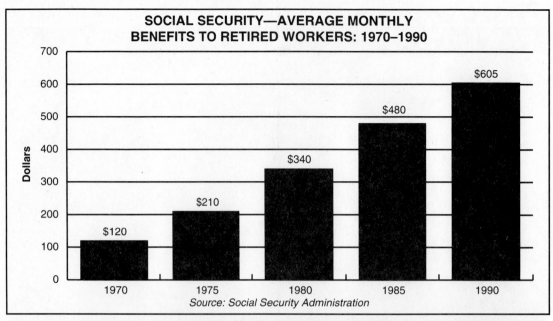

**SOCIAL SECURITY—AVERAGE MONTHLY
BENEFITS TO RETIRED WORKERS: 1970–1990**

Source: Social Security Administration

PART ONE

24. During which year shown did the average benefits for a retired worker equal about $200?

25. What was the approximate monthly benefit payment to retired workers in 1980?

PART TWO

26. On the average, how much more did retired workers receive per month from social security benefits during 1990 than they received during 1985?

27. About what fraction of the amount of 1980 benefits to retired workers is the 1970 amount?

(1) $\frac{1}{4}$ **(2)** $\frac{1}{3}$ **(3)** $\frac{1}{2}$ **(4)** $\frac{3}{4}$

◼ GED Practice ◼
PART THREE

28. By what approximate percentage did average benefits increase between 1985 and 1990?

(1) 15%   **(2)** 25%   **(3)** 40%   **(4)** 55%   **(5)** 75%

29. In 1990, Dorothy Evans paid $262 each month for rent, and she received $50 more per month in social security benefits than the national average shown above. What percentage of her benefits went for rent?

(1) 25%   **(2)** 30%   **(3)** 35%   **(4)** 40%   **(5)** 45%

30. If average benefits increase between the years 1990 and 2010 by the same percentage they increased between 1970 and 1990, what will be the approximate monthly benefits paid in the year 2010?

(1) $1080   **(2)** $1210   **(3)** $2040   **(4)** $3025   **(5)** $4180

ANSWERS ARE ON PAGE 101.

Questions 31–36 refer to the bar graph below.

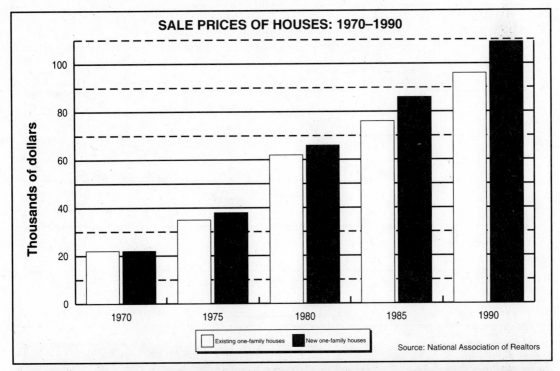

PART ONE

31. What was the approximate average price of a new one-family house in 1990?

32. In what year was the average price of an existing one-family house about $62,000?

PART TWO

33. If Alex Linder had a house built in 1990 at a cost of $150,000, how much more did he pay than the average price of new houses that year?

(1) $4000   **(2)** $9000   **(3)** $41,000   **(4)** $54,000   **(5)** $59,000

34. What is the approximate ratio of the price of a new one-family house built in 1990 to one built in 1970?

(1) 2 to 1   **(2)** 3 to 1   **(3)** 4 to 1   **(4)** 5 to 1   **(5)** 6 to 1

GED Practice

PART THREE

35. What was the approximate percent increase in the average price of an existing one-family house between 1985 and 1990?

(1) 15%   **(2)** 25%   **(3)** 35%   **(4)** 45%   **(5)** 55%

36. If the price of new houses increases at the same percentage rate between 1990 and 2010 as it did between 1970 and 1990, what will be the approximate average cost of a new house in 2010?

(1) $196,000   **(2)** $327,000   **(3)** $436,000   **(4)** $545,000   **(5)** $654,000

ANSWERS ARE ON PAGE 101.

Questions 37–42 refer to the following line graph.

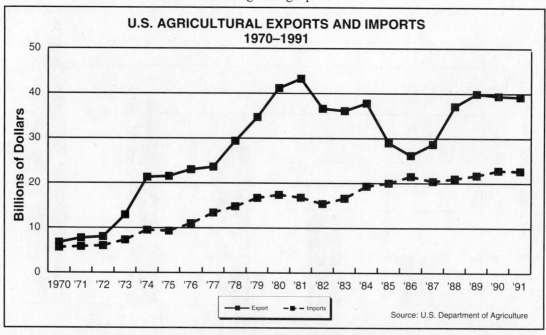

PART ONE

37. What was the approximate value of agricultural *imports* to the United States in 1991?

38. During which year did agricultural exports reach their maximum value?

PART TWO

39. In which of the years shown was the value of agricultural exports most nearly equal to the value of imports?

40. In billions of dollars, what was the approximate difference between the values of exports and imports in 1980?

    (1) 12   **(2)** 17   **(3)** 24   **(4)** 30   **(5)** 35

GED Practice
PART THREE

41. What is the approximate ratio of the value of agricultural exports to imports in 1991?

    (1) 1 to 2   **(2)** 2 to 1   **(3)** 3 to 1   **(4)** 3 to 4   **(5)** 5 to 4

42. What is the approximate percentage increase in the value of agricultural exports between 1985 and 1990?

    (1) 33%   **(2)** 50%   **(3)** 100%   **(4)** 150%   **(5)** 200%

ANSWERS ARE ON PAGE 102.

Questions 43–47 refer to the following graph.

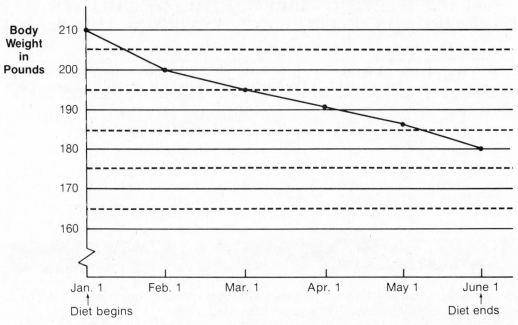

RESULTS OF COLBY'S DIET—January 1–June 1

PART ONE

43. How much did Colby weigh when he started his diet?

PART TWO

44. How many pounds did Colby lose between January 1 and March 1?

45. How many pounds did Colby lose during the 3rd and 4th months of his diet?

GED Practice
PART THREE

46. What fraction of his body weight did Colby lose between January 1 and June 1?

(1) $\frac{1}{4}$ (2) $\frac{1}{5}$ (3) $\frac{1}{6}$ (4) $\frac{1}{7}$ (5) $\frac{1}{8}$

47. What was Colby's average weight loss in pounds per month between January 1 and June 1?

(1) 5   (2) 6   (3) 9   (4) 15   (5) 30

ANSWERS ARE ON PAGE 102.

Questions 48–52 refer to the following table.

<table>
<tr><th colspan="6">AVERAGE TELEVISION VIEWING TIME OF CHILDREN
AND TEENAGERS IN SELECTED WEEKLY VIEWING TIME SLOTS
(in hours and minutes)</th></tr>
<tr><th>GROUP</th><th>AGES</th><th>Mon.-Fri.
10 am-4:30 pm</th><th>Mon.-Fri.
4:30 pm-7:30 pm</th><th>Mon.-Sun.
8-11 pm</th><th>Sat.
7 am-1 pm</th></tr>
<tr><td>Children</td><td>2–5</td><td>6:20</td><td>5:00</td><td>4:44</td><td>2:11</td></tr>
<tr><td></td><td>6–11</td><td>2:19</td><td>5:04</td><td>6:03</td><td>2:01</td></tr>
<tr><td>Teens</td><td></td><td></td><td></td><td></td><td></td></tr>
<tr><td> Females</td><td>13–19</td><td>2:38</td><td>3:56</td><td>6:33</td><td>:49</td></tr>
<tr><td> Males</td><td>13–19</td><td>2:03</td><td>4:11</td><td>6:41</td><td>:59</td></tr>
</table>

Source: Statistical Abstract of the U.S., 1986

PART ONE

48. On the average, how much television do children between the ages of 2 and 5 watch on Saturday morning from 7:00 A.M. to 1:00 P.M.?

49. In which time slot do teenage males watch an average of 4 hours 11 minutes of television?

PART TWO

50. How much total time on the average do children between the ages of 2 and 5 watch television each week during all the time slots shown?

(1) 11 hours 25 minutes   **(4)** 18 hours 15 minutes
(2) 13 hours 45 minutes   **(5)** 21 hours 35 minutes
(3) 16 hours 25 minutes

=== GED Practice ===
PART THREE

51. What is the average of the times that male and female teenagers watch television on Saturday morning from 7:00 A.M. to 1:00 P.M.?

(1) 49 minutes   **(4)** 1 hour 48 minutes
(2) 54 minutes   **(5)** Not enough information is given.
(3) 59 minutes

52. What is the average amount of time that children between the ages of 6 and 11 watch television on Sunday night from 8:00 P.M. to 11:00 P.M.?

(1) 44 minutes   **(4)** 6 hours 3 minutes
(2) 1 hour 23 minutes   **(5)** Not enough information is given.
(3) 2 hours 57 minutes

ANSWERS ARE ON PAGE 102.

Questions 53–58 refer to the following table.

TEN LARGEST METROPOLITAN POPULATION CENTERS IN THE WORLD *(population given in millions)*			
1992		**2000 (projected)**	
1. Tokyo–Yokohama, Japan	27.5	1. Tokyo–Yokohama, Japan	30.0
2. Mexico City, Mexico	21.6	2. Mexico City, Mexico	27.9
3. São Paulo, Brazil	19.4	3. São Paulo, Brazil	25.4
4. Seoul, South Korea	17.3	4. Seoul, South Korea	22.0
5. New York City, United States	14.6	5. Bombay, India	15.4
6. Osaka–Kobe–Kyoto, Japan	13.9	6. New York, United States	14.6
7. Bombay, India	12.5	7. Osaka–Kobe–Kyoto, Japan	14.3
8. Calcutta, India	12.1	8. Rio de Janeiro, Brazil	14.2
9. Rio de Janeiro, Brazil	12.0	9. Calcutta, India	14.1
10. Buenos Aires, Argentina	11.7	10. Buenos Aires, Argentina	12.9

Source: U.S. Bureau of the Census, International Database

PART ONE

53. Which city is projected to be the eighth largest population center in the world in the year 2000?

PART TWO

54. If the projected increases are correct, which of the top five cities in 1992 will no longer be among the top five in 2000?

55. Which of the cities shown is expected to have the same population in 2000 as in 1992?

56. By how many people is the population of Rio de Janeiro projected to increase between 1992 and 2000?

GED Practice
PART THREE

57. By about what percent is the population of São Paulo projected to increase between 1992 and 2000?

(1) 10%   **(2)** 20%   **(3)** 30%   **(4)** 40%   **(5)** 50%

58. Of the following metropolitan centers, which is projected to experience the greatest numerical population increase between 1992 and 2000?

(1) Tokyo–Yokohama   **(4)** Seoul
(2) Mexico City   **(5)** Bombay
(3) São Paulo

ANSWERS ARE ON PAGE 102.

The Basics of Algebra

PART ONE

Directions: Match each algebraic expression below with its equivalent word expression. Write the letter of the matching word expression on the line to the left of each algebraic expression.

Algebraic Expressions

_____ **1.** $\frac{6}{x}$

_____ **2.** $7 - n$

_____ **3.** $-\frac{1}{3}z$

_____ **4.** $n - 7$

_____ **5.** $12y$

_____ **6.** $\frac{x}{6}$

_____ **7.** $\frac{y}{12}$

_____ **8.** $a + 3$

Equivalent Word Expressions

a. n decreased by the number seven

b. the number y divided by twelve

c. the sum of the number a and three

d. x divided by six

e. six divided by the number x

f. negative one-third times the number z

g. seven decreased by the number n

h. twelve times the number y

Directions: Write an algebraic expression for each word expression below.

9. A number n subtracted from fourteen

10. Five times a number x

11. The sum of m and thirty-two

12. Twenty divided by a number i

13. A number b multiplied by nine

14. Fifteen plus a number r

Directions: Find the value of each algebraic expression below.

15. $y + 5$ for $y = 3$

16. $w - 8$ for $w = 16$

17. $6n$ for $n = 4$

18. $\frac{1}{2}x$ for $x = 12$

19. $\frac{q}{8}$ for $q = 48$

20. $\frac{12}{x}$ for $x = 2$

Directions: Write the following algebraic expressions.

21. The Brennans pay a monthly rent of $690. In June their rent goes up an additional n dollars per month. Write an algebraic expression for their June rent.

22. If 8 pounds of potatoes cost n dollars, what is an algebraic expression for the cost of one pound?

23. Ernie is 5 years older than his brother Bert. If Bert's age is represented by the letter x, what algebraic expression represents Ernie's age?

24. The Johnsons are able to save two-fifteenths of their monthly income. Write an algebraic expression representing the amount of the Johnsons' monthly savings. Use i to represent their monthly income.

ANSWERS ARE ON PAGE 102.

Directions: For each equation below, test the proposed solution. If the proposed solution is correct, circle *Yes*; if it is incorrect, circle *No*.

25. $x + 9 = 4$ Try $x = 5$ Yes   No

26. $y - 4 = 13$ Try $y = 9$ Yes   No

27. $3n = 27$ Try $n = 9$ Yes   No

28. $\frac{y}{4} = 24$ Try $y = 6$ Yes   No

Directions: Use the distance and cost formulas to solve the following problems.

29. Connie ran up a total of $6.80 in charges for school lunches. If each one costs $.85, how many school lunches has Connie charged?

30. At an after-Christmas sale, Lee paid only $18.96 for a dozen pair of socks. At this price, how much did Lee pay for each pair?

31. What distance can Kevin drive in six hours if he averages fifty-five miles per hour?

32. To travel a distance of 540 miles in $4\frac{1}{2}$ hours, what average speed would a train need to maintain?

33. Audrey averaged 52 miles per hour as she drove from Salem to Evans, a distance of 182 miles. If she didn't stop along the way, how long did this trip take Audrey?

34. At a grocer's sale, cucumbers were $1.19 a dozen. At this rate, how much will twenty-four cucumbers cost?

ANSWERS FOR PART ONE ARE ON PAGE 102.

PART TWO

Directions: Solve and check each equation below.

1. $x - 13 = 25$ **4.** $\frac{y}{7} = 7$

2. $y + 3 = 9$ **5.** $x + \frac{2}{3} = 2\frac{1}{3}$

3. $4n = 24$ **6.** $n - 6 = 0$

Directions: Write an equation to represent each statment. Then solve the equation for the unknown number.

7. Six plus a number is fourteen.

8. Thirteen less than a number is four.

9. Twenty times a number is equal to one hundred sixty.

10. The quotient of a number divided by four is nine.

Directions: Set up and solve an equation for each of the following problems.

11. After paying the clerk, Jess received $13 in change. If he purchased a pillow for $7, how much money did he give the clerk?

12. Vanessa bought 3 pounds of broccoli for $1.47. What price per pound did Vanessa pay?

13. At a Christmas sale, Vinney bought a jacket marked $25 off. If Vinney had to pay only $34.95, what was the original price of the jacket?

14. Joan spends two-sevenths of her monthly income on food. If Joan's monthly income is $1470, what amount does she spend for food?

15. Georgia earns a commission of 6% on each sale of furniture she makes. During the month of April, Georgia earned $507 in commissions. What was her total sales amount during that month?

16. Alfredo sold his house for $16,500 more than he paid for it ten years ago. If he bought it for $72,000, at what price did he sell it?

Directions: Solve each of the following equations.

17. $8x + 5 = 45$

18. $4y - 9 = 27$

19. $\frac{c}{2} + 3 = 6$

20. $14 = 8z + 6$

21. $26 = 2x - 14$

22. $\frac{1}{4}n - 12 = 0$

23. $2(x + 6) = 20$

24. $5(y - 2) = 15$

25. $24 = 3(n - 3)$

Directions: Set up and solve an equation for each problem below.

26. There are three times as many women shoppers in Jason's Market on Saturdays as there are men. On a Saturday when 360 people came into the store, how many of them were men?

27. Shauna is now 4 years older than her sister Stacey. Two years ago, Shauna was three times as old as Stacey was. How old is each girl now?

28. Erin has two part-time jobs. She earns twice as much each month at Burger Palace as she does baby-sitting. If her total income during July was $636, how much did she earn from baby-sitting?

Directions: Use formulas to solve the following problems. A page listing all algebra and geometry formulas can be found on the inside back cover.

29. If Sal borrowed $1500 for 2 years at a rate of 14% simple interest, how much interest would he owe?

30. What total amount will Kathy have in her savings account after three years if she deposits $500 and the account pays 2.5% simple interest?

ANSWERS ARE ON PAGE 102.

GED Practice
PART THREE

Directions: Solve the following problems. Use the formulas on the inside back cover whenever necessary.

1. Harvey earns a monthly salary of $550 and receives an additional commission of $14 on each suit he sells. During June, Harvey earned a total of $1278. How many suits did Harvey sell in June?

   (1) 14   **(2)** 28   **(3)** 39   **(4)** 52   **(5)** 728

2. If the sum of three consecutive whole numbers is 30, what is the smallest of these numbers?

   (1) 3   **(4)** 12
   (2) 9   **(5)** Not enough information is given.
   (3) 10

3. Every Monday, Wednesday, and Friday, Tomaz jogs around Newman Park. Each Tuesday and Thursday, he jogs around City Reservoir, a distance twice as far as the Newman Park run. If Tomaz jogs a total of 21 miles each week, which equation below can be used to find d, the distance in miles around Newman Park?

   (1) $3(d) - 2(2d) = 21$ **(4)** $(3 - 2)(2d) = 21$
   (2) $3(d) + 2(2d) = 21$ **(5)** $5(d + 2d) = 21$
   (3) $(3 + 2)(2d) = 21$

Questions 4–6 refer to the following information.

> Mary, Paula, and Lillian are partners in a house-cleaning business.
> By mutual agreement, Mary receives $4.00, Paula receives $3.50, and
> Lillian receives $2.50 out of each $10.00 the business earns.

4. Which expression can be used to compute the ratio of the money Mary earns to the money Lillian earns?

   (1) $\frac{(4 - 2.5)}{10}$ **(2)** $\frac{(10 + 4)}{(10 + 2.5)}$ **(3)** $\frac{(10 - 4)}{(10 - 2.5)}$ **(4)** $\frac{2.5}{4}$ **(5)** $\frac{4}{2.5}$

5. How much money did Paula make (in dollars) during a month when the business earned $2400?

   (1) 400   **(2)** 685   **(3)** 800   **(4)** 840   **(5)** 1200

6. During May, Mary earned $630. Which equation below can be used to compute the total monthly receipts (R) of the house-cleaning business during May?

   (1) $630 = \frac{4}{10}R$ **(4)** $630 = \frac{R}{4}$
   (2) $630 = (4)(10)R$ **(5)** $630 = (10 + 4)R$
   (3) $630 = (10 - 4)R$

ANSWERS ARE ON PAGE 103.

7. In 9 months Ray was able to earn $125 from a savings account that pays interest at a rate of 2% per year. Which expression below determines Ray's principal, the amount of money he originally placed in the account?

    (1) $\dfrac{125}{(.02)(.75)}$ **(2)** $\dfrac{125}{(.02)(9)}$ **(3)** $\dfrac{125}{(.2)(.75)}$ **(4)** $\dfrac{125}{(.2)(9)}$ **(5)** $\dfrac{125}{(2)(.75)}$

8. There are nineteen more men than women in Murray's welding class. One-third of the whole class are students under the age of 30. If 75 students are in this welding class, how many of the students are men?

    (1) 10 **(2)** 27 **(3)** 30 **(4)** 45 **(5)** 47

9. Celia deposited $1000 in a savings account in which she earns interest at a rate of 3% per year. How long, in years, will this amount take to earn $22.50 in interest?

    (1) $\frac{1}{2}$ year **(2)** $\frac{3}{4}$ year **(3)** 1 year **(4)** $1\frac{3}{4}$ years **(5)** 2 years

10. To help finance her purchase of a $6000 used car, Virginia borrowed $4000 from Thrifty Finance. She agreed to pay back the entire amount she owed in one payment at the end of seven months. She borrowed the money at a simple interest rate of 13%. Which expression below represents the amount Virginia will have to pay back to Thrifty Finance?

    (1) $(4000)(.13)(\frac{7}{12})$

    (2) $(6000)(.13)(\frac{7}{12})$

    (3) $4000 + (4000)(.13)(\frac{12}{7})$

    (4) $4000 + (4000)(.13)(\frac{7}{12})$

    (5) $6000 + (6000)(.13)(\frac{7}{12})$

Questions 11–13 are based on the following information.

   On Monday, the first day of his trip to San Francisco, Lennie drove 212 miles in 4 hours before stopping for lunch at 12:30 P.M. After lunch, he drove until 7:00 that evening, at which time he stopped for dinner and to get a good night's sleep. Tuesday morning, he drove an average of 50 miles per hour and was able to make San Francisco in just 2 hours and 20 minutes.

11. What average speed in miles per hour did Lennie drive Monday morning before he stopped for lunch?

    (1) 48 **(4)** 58
    (2) 51 **(5)** Not enough information is given.
    (3) 53

12. What more do you need to know in order to determine the total distance that Lennie drove on Monday?

    A. the time Lennie started his trip
    B. the distance Lennie drove after lunch
    C. the time Lennie spent at lunch

    (1) A only **(4)** A and B only
    (2) B only **(5)** B and C only
    (3) C only

ANSWERS ARE ON PAGE 103.

13. About how many miles was Lennie from San Francisco when he started driving Tuesday morning?

(1) 82
(2) 97
(3) 107

(4) 117
(5) Not enough information is given.

14. Each month, Monty spends $\frac{1}{4}$ of his monthly take-home pay for his car payment. If his monthly rent is $285 and his car payment is $212, how much is Monty's monthly take-home pay?

(1) $53   **(2)** $106   **(3)** $212   **(4)** $424   **(5)** $848

15. During the high school basketball game, Mel scored 18 points. Unfortunately, the other team ended up with 79 points and won the game. If Mel scored $\frac{2}{7}$ of the team's total points that night, what was his team's final score?

(1) 57
(2) 63
(3) 68

(4) 69
(5) Not enough information is given.

16. Harry bought a 10-speed bike on sale and then received a $15.00 rebate from the bike company. Harry's final cost was $74.00 for a bike that the store normally sells for $139.50. Before the rebate, what was the sale price of the bike in the store?

(1) $59.00
(2) $65.60
(3) $74.00

(4) $89.00
(5) Not enough information is given.

17. Jerry, Frank, and Scott share food expenses each month. Because he eats only one meal a day at home, Jerry pays $75 less each month than either Frank or Scott. Scott and Frank pay equal amounts. If last month's total food bill came to $411, what was Jerry's share?

(1) $68   **(2)** $87   **(3)** $93   **(4)** $104   **(5)** $112

18. For every dollar his wife earns, Mr. Jameson earns $1.50. If they earn a combined salary of $3050 each month, what is Mrs. Jameson's monthly income?

(1) $610
(2) $1220
(3) $1830

(4) $2287
(5) Not enough information is given.

19. For every four people who ordered sausage pizza at a local restaurant last weekend, one person ordered pepperoni. If 540 people ordered pizza with one of these two toppings, how many people ordered pepperoni?

(1) 32
(2) 108
(3) 120

(4) 180
(5) Not enough information is given.

20. Which of the following is the same as $x^2 + 17x$?

(1) $17x$

(2) $(x + 17)(x - 17)$

(3) $x(1 + 17)$

(4) $\frac{x + 17}{x}$

(5) $x(x + 17)$

ANSWERS ARE ON PAGE 103.

Geometry

PART ONE

1. What is the largest angle of the angles shown below?

A

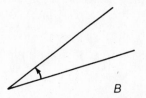

B

C

2. Name each of the geometrical figures shown below.

 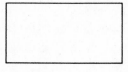

a._____ **b.**_____ **c.**_____ **d.**_____

Directions: For problems 3–18, use the formulas on the inside back cover whenever necessary.

3. Determine the perimeter of each of the fields shown below. Simplify your answers.

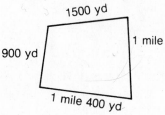 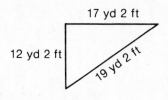 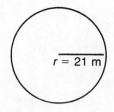

a._____ **b.**_____ **c.**_____

Directions: Determine the value of each of the following expressions.

4. 5^1

5. 2^3

6. 3^3

7. 10^2

8. $(\frac{1}{3})^2$

9. 0.004^2

ANSWERS ARE ON PAGE 104.

10. Determine the area of each of the figures below.

A

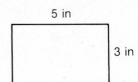

5 in

3 in

B

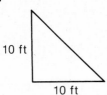

10 ft

10 ft

C

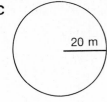

20 m

11. Kelvin is putting new tile on his shop floor. If the rectangular shop is 26 feet long and 18 feet wide, how many square feet of tile will Kelvin need?

12. How many square yards of carpet will it take to carpet the living room floor shown at right?

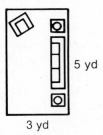

5 yd

3 yd

13. Determine the volume of each figure below.

A

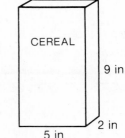

CEREAL

9 in

5 in

2 in

B

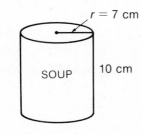

r = 7 cm

SOUP

10 cm

C

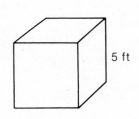

5 ft

14. Jill's sandbox is 6 feet long, 7 feet wide, and $1\frac{1}{2}$ feet deep. How many cubic feet of sand will it take to fill this sandbox?

15. Determine the volume of a shipping container that is in the shape of a cube $1\frac{1}{2}$ yards on an edge.

16. How many cubic inches of water can the aquarium pictured at right hold when completely full?

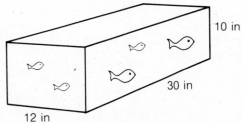

10 in

30 in

12 in

17. Find the value of each angle indicated below.

A

37°

x

∠x =

B

40°

90°

a

∠a =

C

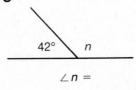

42°

n

∠n =

D

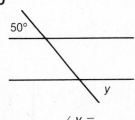

50°

y

∠y =

ANSWERS ARE ON PAGE 104.

18. In the roof gable shown at right, determine the value of the angle indicated by the question mark.

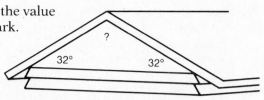

ANSWERS FOR PART ONE BEGIN ON PAGE 104.

PART TWO

Directions: Solve the following problems using the formulas on the inside back cover whenever necessary.

1. Shelley plans to install a fence around her square garden. If each side is 37 feet long and she plans to leave one 3-foot opening for a gate, how many feet of fencing material will she need?

2. As shown in the drawing at right, Charlie is placing oak molding around the outer edge of his bathroom mirror. Assuming no waste, what is the area of molding he will need?

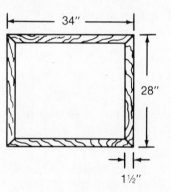

3. The lawn in the front of Pat's house is in the shape of a rectangle that is twice as long as it is wide. What is the distance around the yard if its length is 48 feet?

Directions: Find the following square roots.

4. $\sqrt{324}$

5. $\sqrt{529}$

6. $\sqrt{729}$

7. $\sqrt{1156}$

8. $\sqrt{1521}$

9. $\sqrt{1849}$

Directions: Find approximate square roots of the following numbers. Round each answer to one decimal place.

10. $\sqrt{6}$

11. $\sqrt{51}$

12. $\sqrt{84}$

13. $\sqrt{60}$

14. $\sqrt{32}$

15. $\sqrt{111}$

ANSWERS ARE ON PAGE 104.

16. A sack of Goodgrow Fertilizer will cover an area of 200 square yards of lawn. If Amy's lawn is a square 40 yards on each side, what fraction of her lawn can six Goodgrow sacks be expected to cover?

17. The Brewster family plans to cover their barbecue patio with ceramic tile. The dimensions of the patio are shown at right. At a cost of $1.50 per square foot of tile, how much will the Brewsters spend for the needed tile?

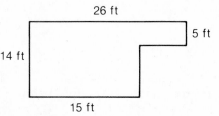

18. Jackie bought a circular rug to place on the floor of her dining room. The floor measures 14 feet long by 11 feet wide. If the diameter of the rug is 10 feet, approximately how many square feet of floor space will be left uncovered?

(1) 55
(2) 65
(3) 75

(4) 85
(5) Not enough information is given.

19. Referring to the drawing at right, what is the ratio of the area of triangle *XYZ* to the area of the rectangle?

(1) $\frac{1}{4}$

(2) $\frac{1}{3}$

(3) $\frac{1}{2}$

(4) $\frac{2}{3}$

(5) Not enough information is given.

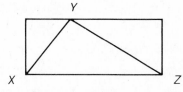

20. A contractor is removing dirt from a hole being dug in the shape of a rectangular solid 3 yards deep, 8 yards long, and 6 yards wide. If each of his trucks can haul 12 cubic yards of dirt, how many truckloads of dirt is the contractor going to remove?

21. How many cubic yards of asphalt will be needed to lay a new 6-inch surface over a section of street that is 6 yards wide and 400 yards long?

22. A water storage tank in the shape of a cylinder is shown at right. If one cubic meter of water weighs one metric ton, approximately how many metric tons of water can the tank hold when full?

(1) 410
(2) 790
(3) 920
(4) 1060
(5) 1230

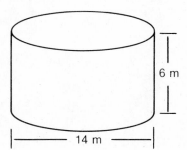

ANSWERS ARE ON PAGE 104.

Questions 23–27 refer to the figure at right.

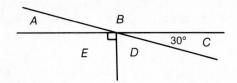

Directions: Match each expression below with its equivalent value. Write the letter of the correct value on the line before each expression.

Expression

_____ **23.** ∠B

_____ **24.** ∠A

_____ **25.** ∠C + ∠D + ∠E

_____ **26.** ∠D

_____ **27.** ∠A + ∠B + ∠C + ∠D + ∠E

Value

a. 30°

b. 180°

c. 360°

d. 60°

e. 150°

28. Elm Street intersects 4th Avenue at an angle of 73° as shown in the drawing at right. If 3rd is parallel to 4th, what are the values of ∠A, ∠B, and ∠C shown in the drawing?

(1) ∠A = 73°, ∠B = 73°, ∠C = 73°
(2) ∠A = 73°, ∠B = 107°, ∠C = 73°
(3) ∠A = 107°, ∠B = 107°, ∠C = 73°
(4) ∠A = 107°, ∠B = 73°, ∠C = 107°
(5) ∠A = 107°, ∠B = 73°, ∠C = 73°

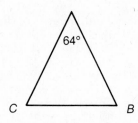

29. What are the values of the two unmeasured angles in the isosceles triangle drawn at right?

(1) ∠B = 61°, ∠C = 58°
(2) ∠B = 58°, ∠C = 58°
(3) ∠B = 61°, ∠C = 61°
(4) ∠B = 58°, ∠C = 61°
(5) ∠B = 60°, ∠C = 60°

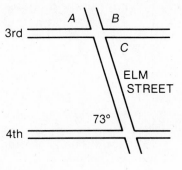

30. Dave estimated the distance across Lewiston Lake by walking off distances and making the drawing at right. Use his drawing to determine the distance across the lake.

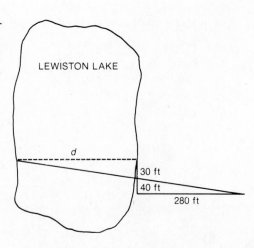

ANSWERS ARE ON PAGE 104.

31. Which of the following pairs of triangles are congruent?

     A   **B**   **C**   **D**

  (1) $\triangle A$ and $\triangle B$ **(4)** $\triangle B$ and $\triangle C$
  (2) $\triangle A$ and $\triangle C$ **(5)** $\triangle B$ and $\triangle D$
  (3) $\triangle A$ and $\triangle D$

32. A hiker leaves Forest Camp and walks directly east for a distance of 8 miles. She then walks directly north an additional 6 miles before stopping to rest. At this point, what is her straight-line distance from Forest Camp?

33. A 50-foot-high tree toppled during a windstorm and is now leaning against the side of Ben's barn. If the bottom of the tree is 48 feet from the side of the barn, at what height above the ground is the tree touching the barn?

34. What is the approximate distance in feet from corner A to corner C of the pool shown at right?

  (1) 22   **(4)** 32
  (2) 26   **(5)** 35
  (3) 29

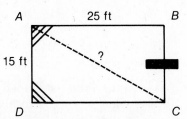

ANSWERS FOR PART TWO BEGIN ON PAGE 104.

GED Practice
PART THREE

Directions: Solve the following problems using the formulas on the inside back cover whenever necessary.

1. Each morning, Monday through Friday, Aaron runs 8 laps around the circular jogging trail in the park. If the trail has a radius of 175 yards, how many miles does Aaron jog each day? Use the value $\pi = \frac{22}{7}$. (1 mile = 1760 yards.)

  (1) 2   **(2)** 3   **(3)** 4   **(4)** 5   **(5)** 6

2. If 88 9-inch-long bricks lie around the edge of a circular garden space, what is the circumference (in feet) of this garden?

  (1) 18   **(2)** 35   **(3)** 42   **(4)** 56   **(5)** 66

3. Which of the following expressions can be used to find the perimeter in yards of the rectangular lawn pictured below?

  (1) $2(32 - 18)$
  (2) $4(32 + 18)$
  (3) $(2)(32) + (2)(18)$
  (4) $(2)(32)(18)$
  (5) $(32)(18)$

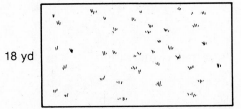

ANSWERS ARE ON PAGE 104.

4. According to the directions on the can, a gallon of wall paint holds 32 cubic inches of liquid and will cover 400 square feet of surface. With no waste, what is the maximum length in feet of an 8-foot-high wall that can be painted with three gallons of paint?

(1) 50 **(2)** 100 **(3)** 150 **(4)** 450 **(5)** 1200

5. The edge of the community wading pool shown at right is lined with side-by-side seats on which children can sit and place their feet in the water. If the seats are three feet apart, which expression below tells approximately how many seats are along the edge of the pool?

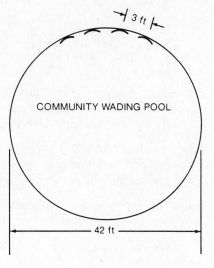

COMMUNITY WADING POOL

3 ft

42 ft

(1) $\dfrac{42}{(3)(\frac{22}{7})}$

(2) $\dfrac{3}{(\frac{22}{7})(42)}$

(3) $\dfrac{(\frac{22}{7})(42)}{3}$

(4) $\dfrac{(2)(\frac{22}{7})(42)}{3}$

(5) $\dfrac{(\frac{22}{7})(21)}{3}$

6. A corner table is shaped like a right triangle. One of the two sides that form the right angle has a length of 3 feet. The next shortest side has a length of 4 feet. How many feet long is the third side of this table?

(1) 5 **(2)** 6 **(3)** 7 **(4)** 9 **(5)** 25

Questions 7–9 refer to the following information.

As indicated by the drawing below, the Robinson family has a garden, a shed, and a patio in their back yard. The rest of the back yard is planted in grass.

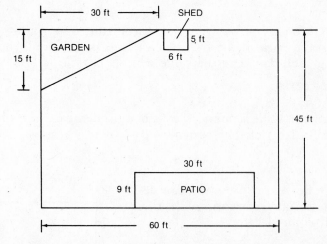

7. What is the ratio of the area of the patio to the area of the garden?

(1) $\frac{3}{10}$ **(2)** $\frac{3}{5}$ **(3)** $\frac{6}{5}$ **(4)** $\frac{2}{1}$ **(5)** $\frac{3}{1}$

ANSWERS ARE ON PAGE 104.

8. What percent of the area of the Robinsons' back yard is used for the patio?

(1) 10   **(2)** 20   **(3)** 27   **(4)** 40   **(5)** 50

9. How many square feet of the back yard are planted in grass?

(1) 2175   **(2)** 2075   **(3)** 1175   **(4)** 1005   **(5)** 995

10. The inside dimensions of Leona's freezer are as follows: length = 5 feet; width = 3 feet; height = 4 feet. What is the maximum number of boxes of frozen fish, each measuring 12 inches × 12 inches × 4 inches, that Leona can store in this freezer?

(1) 15   **(2)** 16   **(3)** 48   **(4)** 60   **(5)** 180

11. Knowing that 1 cubic foot is equal to about 7.5 gallons, what is the approximate number of gallons of water that can be held in the water bed pictured at right?

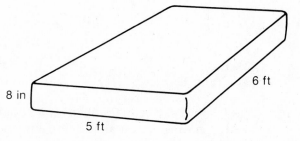

8 in   5 ft   6 ft

(1) 105
(2) 150
(3) 165
(4) 180
(5) 1800

12. Dotty wants to fertilize her rectangular yard, which measures 28 yards long by 15 yards wide. She plans to use a fertilizer that costs $3.49 for a bag that covers thirty square yards. How much money (in dollars) will Dotty need to spend on the fertilizer, not including tax?

(1) $6.98   **(2)** $14.00   **(3)** $48.86   **(4)** $104.70   **(5)** $420.00

13. As shown at right, a hollow metal tube has an outside diameter of 18 inches and an inner diameter of 16 inches. Which of the following expressions represents the number of cubic inches of metal contained in each 1-inch length of this tube?

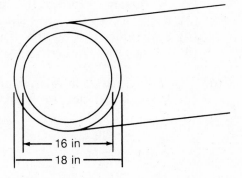

16 in   18 in

(1) $(3.14)(9 + 8)$
(2) $(3.14)(9^2 + 8^2)$
(3) $(3.14)(9 - 8)$
(4) $(3.14)(9 - 8)^2$
(5) $(3.14)(9^2 - 8^2)$

14. Beginning at 9:00 A.M. on Saturday, Albany High School is draining the school swimming pool. The pool holds 15,400 cubic feet of water, and drains at the rate of 100 gallons per minute. What additional information do you need to know to determine the time at which the pool will be empty?

(1) the number of hours it takes to fill the pool
(2) the length and width of the pool
(3) the size of the drain
(4) the number of gallons in one cubic foot
(5) the average depth of the pool

ANSWERS ARE ON PAGE 105.

15. According to the Pythagorean theorem, which of the following statements is true for the triangle in the drawing at right?

(1) $c^2 + 2^2 = b^2$
(2) $b^2 + c^2 = 2^2$
(3) $c^2 - b^2 = 2^2$
(4) $b^2 - c^2 = 2^2$
(5) $2^2 - b^2 = c^2$

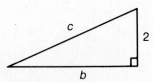

16. Which of the following expressions has (have) the value 8?

A. 2^2
B. 2^4
C. 4^2
D. 8^0
E. 8^1

(1) C only
(2) E only
(3) C and E

(4) B, C, D, E
(5) A, B, C, D, E

17. The Eversweet Sugar Company packs sugar cubes in cubical boxes that measure twelve centimeters on a side. If each sugar cube measures one centimeter on a side, how many cubes can be placed in each box?

(1) 12   (2) 36   (3) 144   (4) 864   (5) 1728

18. Frank is worried that a nearby tree may topple onto his house during the next winter. To see if this could happen, Frank decides to measure the tree's height. At 10:00 one morning he notices that a yardstick casts a shadow of 4 feet 5 inches. What else must Frank know to be able to determine the height of the tree?

(1) the angle of the sun over the horizon
(2) the distance between the yardstick and the tree
(3) the length of the tree's shadow
(4) the diameter of the tree
(5) the distance of the tree from the house

19. Together with the information given in the drawing at right, which of the following conditions is sufficient to ensure that triangle *LMN* is congruent to triangle *RST*?

A. $\angle M = 80°$
B. $\angle T = 60°$
C. $RT = 3$ feet

(1) A only
(2) B only
(3) C only
(4) A or B
(5) B or C

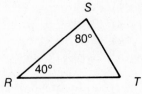

20. Which of the following expressions has the largest value?

(1) $3^2 - 2^0$
(2) $9^0 - 1^4$
(3) $4^2 - 3^2$

(4) $3^3 - 5^2$
(5) $9^1 - 0^5$

ANSWERS ARE ON PAGE 105.

21. Find the area in square inches of the figure at right.

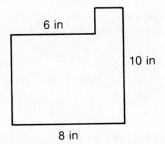

    (1) 40
    (2) 48
    (3) 60
    (4) 480
    (5) Not enough information is given.

22. One side of a square measures eight meters. A rectangle with the same area as the square has a length of sixteen meters. How many meters wide is the rectangle?

    (1) 2   **(4)** 6
    (2) 2.5   **(5)** Not enough information is given.
    (3) 4

ANSWERS ARE ON PAGE 106.

Special Topics in Algebra and Geometry

PART ONE

Questions 1–8 refer to the following number line.

```
      A    B        C   D   E       F G
   ┴──┴──┴──┴──┴──┴──┴──┴──┴──┴──┴
  -4  -3  -2  -1   0   1   2   3   4
```

1. What is the value of the number represented by the letter *E*?

2. What is the value of the number represented by the letter *C*?

3. What letter on the number line represents the number 2.5?

4. What letter on the number line represents the number −2.75?

5. What is the sum of the two numbers represented by the letters *A* and *G*?

6. What is the sum of the two numbers represented by the letters *A* and *D*?

7. How much larger is the number represented by the letter *G* than the number represented by the letter *A*?

8. What is the difference between the two numbers represented by the letters *C* and *G*?

Directions: In problems 9–16, solve each problem as indicated.

9. $-4 + 8 =$

10. $-9 + (-5) =$

11. $12 - (-6) =$

12. $-13 - (-6) =$

13. $-3 + (-10) =$

14. $(-5)(-6) =$

15. $(-7)(+3) =$

16. $\frac{-9}{-3} =$

17. The top of Mount Everest, the highest mountain on earth, is 29,028 feet above sea level. The bottom of the Kermadec Trench in the Pacific Ocean is 32,809 feet below sea level. What is the difference in height between the top of Mount Everest and the bottom of the Kermadec Trench?

18. At 4:00 P.M., the Chicago temperature was 7°C. By 9:00 that night, the temperature had dropped to −4°C. By how many degrees did the temperature drop between 4:00 P.M. and 9:00 P.M.?

19. What is the difference in temperature recorded on the two thermometers shown at right?

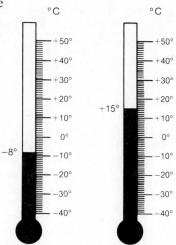

20. While scuba diving, Maria dove to the ocean bottom, 125 feet below sea level. As she came back up to the surface, she saw a baby shark swimming at a depth of 76 feet. At this point, how far was Maria from the ocean bottom?

21. Solve for x in $x - 2 > 5$

22. Solve for n in $3n < 9$

23. Solve for z in $4z \geq -2$

24. Write the following inequality in mathematical symbols: "seven x is less than or equal to minus six."

25. Write the following inequality in mathematical symbols: "negative four is greater than or equal to the number n."

ANSWERS FOR PART ONE BEGIN ON PAGE 106.

PART TWO

Directions: Solve the following problems using the formulas on the inside back cover whenever necessary.

1. Referring to the number line below, which ordering lists from smallest to largest the numbers represented by letters?

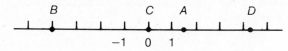

(1) *A, B, C, D*   (4) *B, C, A, D*
(2) *B, A, C, D*   (5) *C, A, D, B*
(3) *D, A, C, B*

2. As a weather balloon slowly rose higher, it measured air temperature. At an altitude of 5 miles, the temperature was $-11°F$, while at 8 miles, it was $-42°F$. By how many degrees did the temperature drop between the altitudes of 5 miles and 8 miles?

3. During the 6 months of his diet, Jeff's weight fluctuated up and down. In January he lost 9 pounds; in February he lost 4 pounds; in March he gained 3 pounds; in April he lost 2 pounds; in May he gained 5 pounds; and in June he lost 4 pounds. If he weighed 208 pounds on January 1, what was Jeff's weight at the end of June?

ANSWERS ARE ON PAGE 106.

4. Willie's checking account balance at the beginning of May was $200. After the following transactions, what is his new balance?

Checks		Deposits	
5/2	$325.00	5/1	$400.00
5/14	110.25	5/16	342.00
5/22	84.00		
5/30	209.85		

5. On January 1, Emma owed a balance of $124.00 on her Shopper's Heaven charge account. During January she made the following payments and charges, and she returned

1/8	Payment	$50.00	1/23	Credit	$25.60
1/14	Charge	34.75	1/23	Charge	18.98
1/18	Charge	4.49	1/24	Credit	12.00
1/19	Payment	75.00	1/30	Charge	9.50

Monthly finance charge $1.65

two items for credit. Including the monthly finance charge, what was the new balance that Emma owed at the end of January?

6. Solve for n in $3n - 5 < 4$

7. Solve for z in $\frac{z}{4} + 3 > 15$

8. Solve for x in $2x - 4 > x + 6$

9. Solve for y in $2(y - 3) \leq y + 1$

10. Which of the following inequalities is *not* true?

(1) $-4 > -2$ **(4)** $6 > -6$

(2) $-7 > -9$ **(5)** $-3 \geq -3$

(3) $3 \geq 0$

11. Which of the following inequalities is true?

(1) $2^3 < 4$ **(4)** $2^3 < 4^2$

(2) $2^3 < 4^0$ **(5)** $2^3 < 4 \times 2$

(3) $2^3 < 4^1$

12. For which value of x below is the inequality $3x < 9$ true?

(1) 2   **(2)** 3   **(3)** 4   **(4)** 5   **(5)** 6

Directions: Multiply or divide each monomial as indicated.

13. $(4x^2)(3x^2) =$

14. $\frac{2}{3}x^2y^3 \cdot 3x^2z^4 =$

15. $x^2x^3x^4 =$

16. $\dfrac{24a^3b^2c}{6a^3b^2} =$

Directions: Simplify the square root in problems 17–20.

17. $\sqrt{50}$

18. $\sqrt{75}$

19. $\sqrt{45}$

20. $\sqrt{500}$

ANSWERS ARE ON PAGE 106.

GED Practice
PART THREE

Directions: Solve the following problems using the formulas on the inside back cover whenever necessary.

1. In three weeks, Ben will have more than 3 times as much money as he has now. If n represents what Ben has now and x represents what he will have in three weeks, which of the following inequalities is true?

   (1) $3n > x$

   (2) $x > n + 3$

   (3) $n > 3x$

   (4) $\frac{x}{3} > \frac{n}{3}$

   (5) $x > 3n$

2. Referring to the points indicated by letters on the number line below, which of the following statements is (are) true?

   A. $M > P$
   B. $N < O < P$
   C. $P < N < M$

   (1) A only
   (2) B only
   (3) C only

   (4) A and C only
   (5) B and C only

3. Letting the letter F represent Fred's age now and J Jimmy's age, which of the following inequalities represents the fact that in four years Fred will be more than twice as old as Jimmy will be?

   (1) $F + 4 > 2J$
   (2) $J + 4 > 2F$
   (3) $J + 4 > 2(F + 4)$

   (4) $F + 4 > 2(J + 4)$
   (5) $F + 4 > 2J + 4$

4. A computer scanning device counts the number of cans being loaded into packing crates. According to company policy, a crate can be shipped as long as it contains at least 138 but no more than 142 cans. When the number of cans loaded into a crate is outside this range, the computer sets off an alarm. If n represents the number of cans in a crate, which of the expressions below can the computer use to determine when to sound the alarm?

   A. $n < 138$
   B. $n > 138$
   C. $138 < n < 142$
   D. $n > 142$

   (1) A and B only
   (2) B only
   (3) A and D only

   (4) C only
   (5) B and D only

5. Which expression below has the same value as $18x - 6$?

   (1) $6(3x) - 1$
   (2) $6(3x - 1)$
   (3) $6x(3x - x)$

   (4) $6x(3x - 1)$
   (5) $6(3x - x)$

ANSWERS ARE ON PAGE 106.

6. Which expression below has the same value as $n^3 - 8n^2$?

   (1) $n^2(n - 8)$ **(4)** $n^2(n - 8n)$
   (2) $3n(n - 8)$ **(5)** $8n^2(n - 1)$
   (3) $(n - 8)(n - 8)$

7. Which of the following most nearly equals in feet the side of a square that has an area of 128 square feet?

   (1) $3\sqrt{7}$ **(4)** $6\sqrt{3}$
   (2) $4\sqrt{7}$ **(5)** $8\sqrt{2}$
   (3) $5\sqrt{3}$

8. The perimeter of a rectangular lawn is 96 yards. If the lawn is three times as long as it is wide, how many yards long is the lawn?

   (1) 8   **(4)** 36
   (2) 12   **(5)** Not enough information is given.
   (3) 24

9. The distance around an empty lot is 810 yards. The lot is in the shape of a rectangle that is 25 yards longer than it is wide. What is the width of this lot in yards?

   (1) 190
                        (4) 234
   (2) $196\frac{1}{4}$
                        (5) Not enough information is given.
   (3) 215

10. The height of triangle *XYZ* is equal to $\frac{1}{2}$ the length of its base. If the area of this triangle is 9 square inches, what is its height in inches?

    (1) 2   **(2)** $2\frac{1}{2}$ **(3)** 3   **(4)** 6   **(5)** 9

11. As shown at right, what is the ratio of the area of rectangle II to rectangle I?

    (1) $\frac{2x}{3y}$

    (2) $6xy$

    (3) $\frac{3}{2}$

    (4) $\frac{6}{1}$

    (5) Not enough information is given.

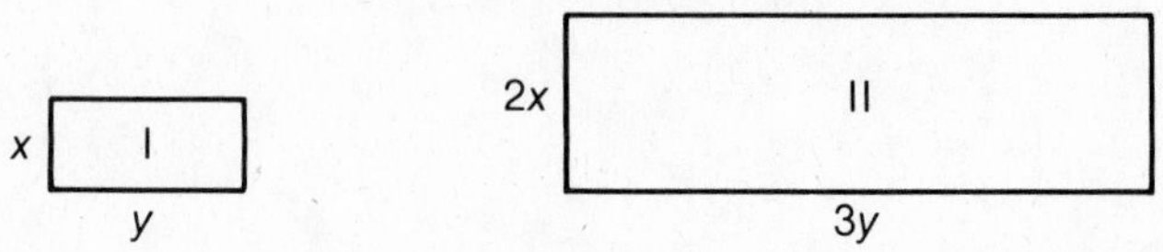

12. Which of the following points is *not* on the graph of the linear equation $y = 4x - 7$?

    (1) $(1,-3)$ **(2)** $(-2,-15)$ **(3)** $(0,-7)$ **(4)** $(3,4)$ **(5)** $(4,9)$

13. What are the *x* and *y* intercepts of the graph of the linear equation $y = -2x + 4$?

    (1) x intercept = 0 y intercept = -4
    (2) x intercept = 2 y intercept = 4
    (3) x intercept = -2 y intercept = 0
    (4) x intercept = 4 y intercept = -2
    (5) x intercept = 4 y intercept = 2

ANSWERS ARE ON PAGE 106.

14. Compute the distance between points
A and B shown on the graph at right.

(1) 1
(2) 9
(3) 10
(4) 15
(5) 21

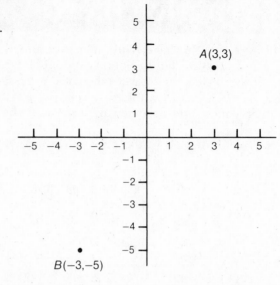

15. What is the slope of the line that passes through the points $(-4,-2)$ and $(6,3)$?

(1) 2

(2) $\frac{1}{2}$

(3) $-\frac{1}{2}$

(4) -2

(5) Not enough information is given.

Directions: In problems 16–17, choose the correct solution to each quadratic equation.

16. $x^2 - 4x - 5 = 0$

(1) $x = 4$ and $x = -5$
(2) $x = 5$ and $x = -1$
(3) $x = 0$ and $x = -4$
(4) $x = 1$ and $x = -5$
(5) $x = 4$ and $x = 0$

17. $y^2 - 7y + 12 = 0$

(1) $y = -7$ and $y = 12$
(2) $y = 3$ and $y = 4$
(3) $y = 1$ and $y = -8$
(4) $y = -3$ and $y = -4$
(5) $y = 3$ and $y = -4$

18. Which of the expressions below computes
the slope of the line connecting points A
and B on the graph at right?

(1) $\frac{4 - (-5)}{-3 - 2}$

(2) $\frac{4 - (-5)}{2 + (-3)}$

(3) $\frac{4 - (-5)}{3 - (-2)}$

(4) $\frac{4 + (-5)}{2 + (-3)}$

(5) $\frac{4 + (-5)}{2 - (-3)}$

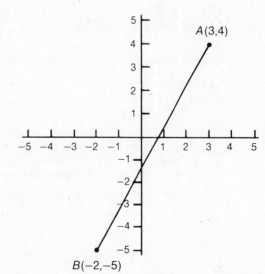

ANSWERS ARE ON PAGE 107.

Practice Test

Directions: You have 90 minutes to complete the following practice test. Try to answer every question, but do not take too much time on any one question. Use the formulas on the inside back cover whenever necessary.

When you are finished, check your answers. The evaluation chart on page 107 will help you determine which areas to review before you take the GED Mathematics Test.

1. As indicated in the illustration below, how far apart are points *A* and *B*?

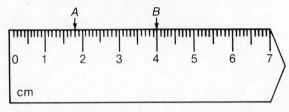

    (1) 2.0 cm   **(2)** 2.2 cm   **(3)** 2.5 cm   **(4)** 3.0 cm   **(5)** 3.2 cm

2. Which of the following word expressions has the same meaning as the algebraic expression $3x - 5$?

    (1) five take away three times a number
    (2) three times a number minus three times five
    (3) three times the difference of a number and five
    (4) three times a number subtracted from five
    (5) five subtracted from three times a number

3. While shopping at Ninth Street Market, Emma bought a "picnic pack" of chicken weighing 9 pounds 15 ounces on sale for $1.02 per pound. Which of the following products gives the best estimate of the amount, in dollars, she will have to pay for this chicken?

    (1) 9×1 **(2)** 9×2 **(3)** 10×1 **(4)** 10×2 **(5)** 24×1

4. If Belinda's family drinks three quarts of milk each day, how much milk does the family drink in a 31-day month?

    (1) 9 gallons 3 quarts   **(4)** 23 gallons 1 quart
    (2) 12 gallons   **(5)** 91 gallons
    (3) 16 gallons 3 quarts

5. Which of the following expressions has the same value as $\dfrac{x^5 y^3}{x^2 y^2}$?

    (1) $x^7 y^5$ **(4)** $x^3 - y$
    (2) $x^3 y$ **(5)** $x^3 y - x^2 y^2$
    (3) $x - y$

6. The term *windchill* refers to the fact that wind causes air temperature to feel much colder than it is. On a day when the thermometer reads $-10°F$, a 20-mile-per-hour wind created a windchill reading of $-53°F$. How much colder was the windchill index than the actual temperature reading?

    (1) 23°F   **(2)** 30°F   **(3)** 33°F   **(4)** 43°F   **(5)** 63°F

ANSWERS ARE ON PAGE 88.

7. Gwen deposited $500 in a State Bank savings account that pays 2.5% simple interest. If she does not add money to or remove money from this account, what will be the amount of her savings in 2 years?

(1) $512.50 **(2)** $525 **(3)** $590 **(4)** $790 **(5)** Not enough information is given.

8. When the price of an Early American style dining room set was lowered from $549 to $439, Harriet bought it. She made a down payment of $79 and agreed to pay the balance and a small finance charge as 8 monthly payments of $49 each. Under these terms, how much in total will Harriet pay for the dining room set?

(1) $392 **(2)** $439 **(3)** $471 **(4)** $493 **(5)** $503

9. Based on the illustration below, which expression represents the fraction of the distance that Woodland is from Walterville to Rosa Bay?

(1) $\frac{120}{168}$ **(2)** $\frac{168}{(168+120)}$ **(3)** $\frac{120}{(168+120)}$ **(4)** $\frac{168}{(168-120)}$ **(5)** $\frac{120}{(168-120)}$

10. Out of his monthly income of $1284, Hubert spends $\frac{1}{6}$ on a car payment, $\frac{1}{4}$ on rent, and $\frac{1}{3}$ on food. After these expenses are taken out, how much of Hubert's income is left?

(1) $218 **(2)** $321 **(3)** $428 **(4)** $642 **(5)** $963

11. Every evening, Curt rides his bicycle six times around Rainbow Lake. The bike path around the lake is approximately in the shape of a circle with a radius of 154 yards. Using the value $\pi \cong \frac{22}{7}$, determine approximately how far Curt rides each evening (1 mile = 1760 yards).

(1) 2.3 miles **(2)** 2.7 miles **(3)** 3.3 miles **(4)** 3.8 miles **(5)** 4.2 miles

12. Starting with a 25-foot ribbon, Sally cut off and saved a piece that measures $8\frac{1}{2}$ feet long. She then divided the remaining piece into several short pieces that were each $2\frac{1}{4}$ feet long. How many of these $2\frac{1}{4}$-foot pieces was Sally able to cut?

(1) 4 **(2)** 5 **(3)** 6 **(4)** 7 **(5)** 8

13. On the first day of the strike, only 35% of the high school teachers were present in their classrooms. If 14 teachers showed up for work that day, how many teachers are employed at the high school?

(1) 21 **(2)** 35 **(3)** 40 **(4)** 49 **(5)** Not enough information is given.

Questions 14–16 refer to the following illustration.

GREEN PINES LUMBER COMPANY
Total Sales Figures for Selected Years

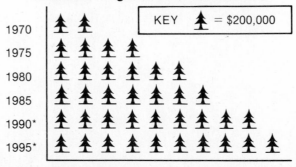

*Projected sales

ANSWERS ARE ON PAGE 88.

14. During which of the reported years did the sales figures of Green Pines Lumber Company first exceed $1,000,000?

    (1) 1970   **(2)** 1975   **(3)** 1980   **(4)** 1985   **(5)** 1995

15. For the first 4 sales figures shown (1970–1985), what is the average amount of sales reported by Green Pines?

    (1) $950,000   **(4)** $1,400,000
    (2) $1,250,000   **(5)** $1,500,000
    (3) $1,300,000

16. For all 6 sales figures shown (including projected figures), what is the median value of sales reported on this graph?

    (1) $900,000   **(4)** $1,700,000
    (2) $1,300,000   **(5)** Not enough information is given.
    (3) $1,500,000

17. For which value of x is the inequality $-3 < x - 1 < 0$ true?

    (1) -3 **(2)** -2 **(3)** 0 **(4)** 1 **(5)** 2

18. How much total interest will Liz be required to pay if she borrows $2500 for 10 months at a simple interest rate of 18%?

    (1) $375   **(2)** $425   **(3)** $450   **(4)** $475   **(5)** $500

19. In his dresser drawer, Henry has 4 pairs of black socks, 3 pairs of dark blue socks, and 2 pairs of dark brown socks. If he reaches into the drawer without looking, what is the probability that in one try he will pick a pair of dark blue socks?

    (1) $\frac{1}{4}$ **(2)** $\frac{1}{3}$ **(3)** $\frac{1}{2}$ **(4)** $\frac{2}{3}$ **(5)** $\frac{3}{4}$

20. Between 9:00 A.M. and 11:00 A.M., Kevin drove at an average speed of 45 miles per hour. Then, between 1:00 P.M. and 4:00 P.M., Kevin drove at an average speed of 60 miles per hour. What is the ratio of the distance Kevin drove in the morning to the distance he drove in the afternoon?

    (1) $\frac{2}{5}$
    (2) $\frac{1}{2}$ **(4)** $\frac{2}{3}$
    (3) $\frac{3}{5}$ **(5)** Not enough information is given.

21. As shown below, a ladder is leaning against the side of Mr. Wong's house. If the ladder makes an angle of 62° with the ground, how many degrees are in the acute angle the ladder makes with the house?

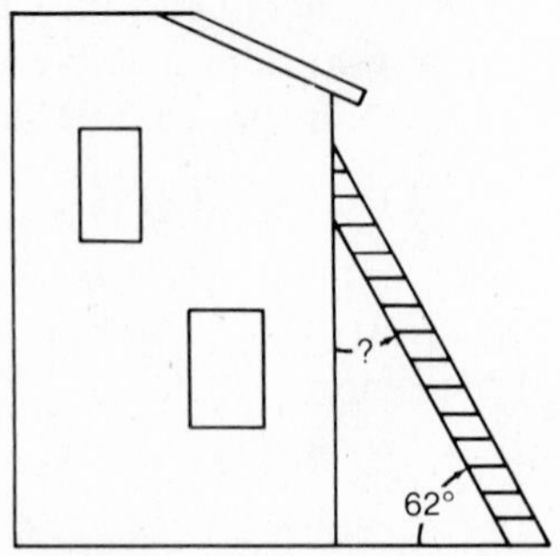

    (1) 28°
    (2) 38°
    (3) 62°
    (4) 90°
    (5) 128°

ANSWERS ARE ON PAGE 88.

22. What speed, in miles per hour, will Arthur need to average if he is to drive the 338 miles between Harrison and Newlin in 6 hours and 30 minutes?

(1) 42 **(2)** 46 **(3)** 49 **(4)** 52 **(5)** 55

23. Kyle's son, Jimmy, plays on the Wildcats summer baseball team. Out of their first 15 games this summer, they won 3 for every 2 they lost. How many of their first 15 games did they win?

(1) 6 **(2)** 7 **(3)** 9 **(4)** 10 **(5)** 12

24. During her first six months as a computer software salesperson, Tanya received a training-level wage of $4.50 per hour. When she completed the training period, her salary increased to $6.30 per hour. By what percent had her salary increased?

(1) 18% **(2)** 25% **(3)** $33\frac{1}{3}$% **(4)** 40% **(5)** 50%

25. Two drainage pipes are joined as shown in the illustration at right. If they join at an acute angle of 50°, what is the value of angle A, the obtuse angle the two pipes make with each other?

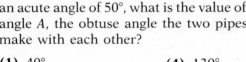

(1) 40° **(4)** 130°
(2) 50° **(5)** 310°
(3) 90°

26. As shown in the illustration below, the Woodside family's backyard is divided into a grassy area and a garden space. How many square yards of grass are contained in their backyard?

WOODSIDE'S BACKYARD

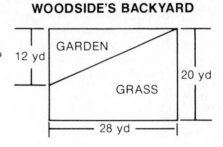

(1) 138 **(4)** 422
(2) 284 **(5)** 448
(3) 392

Questions 27–29 refer to the following situation.

When the Kramers rented a house, they agreed with the owner to pay the following on the day they move in: the first month's rent of $430; a cleaning deposit of $280—$150 of which is refundable if the house is clean when the Kramers move out; a security deposit of $400—fully refundable if no damage is done to the house. The owner will pay the Kramers 6% simple interest on their deposits from the day they move in until the day they move out.

27. How much total cash must the Kramers pay the owners on the day they move into the house?

(1) $560 **(2)** $710 **(3)** $830 **(4)** $960 **(5)** $1110

28. How much interest will the Kramers' cleaning and security deposits earn each month they rent the house?

(1) $2.75 **(4)** $5.50
(2) $2.90 **(5)** Not enough information is given.
(3) $3.40

ANSWERS ARE ON PAGE 89.

29. The Kramers stayed for 10 months, and, before moving out, they did a good job of cleaning. Unfortunately, one of the children damaged the front door, and the Kramers did not repair it. The owner had to pay $75 for new glass and had to pay a repairman to install it. Adding in the interest earned, how much of the deposits can the Kramers reasonably expect the owner to refund?

(1) $475

(2) $509

(3) $605

(4) $639

(5) Not enough information is given.

30. Jill can type at the rate of 65 words per minute. Which of the following equations can be used to determine the number of minutes (t) it would take Jill to type a report that contains 2840 words?

(1) $t - 65 = 2840$

(2) $t + 65 = 2840$

(3) $\frac{t}{65} = 2840$

(4) $2840t = 65$

(5) $65t = 2840$

31. After lowering the price of the large order of popcorn from $2.25 to $1.75, the Twelfth Street Cinema had a 30% increase in the number of large popcorns sold. Before the price reduction, the cinema sold an average of 70 large popcorns each evening. How many sales do they average now?

(1) 73   **(2)** 79   **(3)** 83   **(4)** 91   **(5)** 98

32. As shown in the drawing at right, Tommy is making a scale model of a sailboat, the partial dimensions of which are labeled. If Tommy wants the mainsail on the model to be 12 inches wide, how many inches tall should he make it?

(1) 15
(2) 18
(3) 21
(4) 24
(5) 27

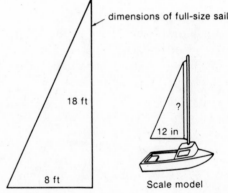

dimensions of full-size sail

18 ft

8 ft

?

12 in

Scale model

The sail angles are identical on full-size sail and on model.

33. For every 7 cartons of plain milk drunk by the students at Osborne Elementary School at lunch, 4 cartons of chocolate milk are drunk. Of the average 462 cartons of milk drunk each day at lunch, how many are chocolate?

(1) 126   **(2)** 168   **(3)** 198   **(4)** 264   **(5)** 294

ANSWERS ARE ON PAGE 89.

Questions 34–35 refer to the illustration below—the sandbox in the children's play area of Walnut Park. In the center of the sandbox is a square built-in toy box in which toys are stored.

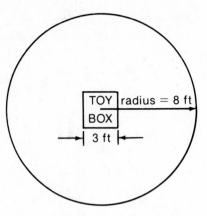

34. Which of the following expressions gives the area, in square feet, of the sand-covered part of the sandbox?

   (1) $\pi 8^2 + 3^2$

   (2) $\pi(8 - 3)^2$

   (3) $\pi 8^2 - 3^2$

   (4) $\pi(8 - 3)^2$

   (5) $2(\pi 8 - 3)^2$

35. Rounded to the nearest whole number, what is the distance, in feet, around the outer edge of the sandbox?

   (1) 45   **(2)** 50   **(3)** 55   **(4)** 60   **(5)** 65

36. When the price of watermelons dropped to \$.17 per pound, Russ bought one that weighed 16 pounds. He also bought 4 pounds of cherries on sale for \$.79 per pound. Which of the following expressions represents the amount of change he should receive if he pays for this purchase with a 10-dollar bill?

   (1) $10 - (16 + 4)(.17 + .79)$

   (2) $10 - (16 + .17)(4 + .79)$

   (3) $10 - 16(.17) + 4(.79)$

   (4) $10 - 16(.17) - 4(.79)$

   (5) $10 - 16(.79) - 4(.17)$

37. As shown in his drawing at right, Pete Peterson is building a patio behind his house. If he makes the patio 6 inches thick, how many cubic yards of concrete will he need?

   (1) 5

   (2) 6

   (3) 7

   (4) 8

   (5) Not enough information is given.

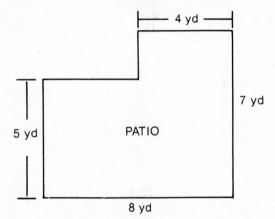

38. Sayuko works a 40-hour shift each week on her job at Future Electronics. She also averages an additional 6 hours of overtime work each week, for which she earns $1\frac{1}{2}$ times her regular hourly rate. If her regular pay is \$6.50 per hour, which of the following expressions represents Sayuko's average weekly income?

   (1) $40(6.5) + 6(\frac{2}{3})(6.5)$

   (2) $40(6.5) + 6(\frac{3}{2})(6.5)$

   (3) $40(6.5) + \dfrac{(6)(6.5)}{\frac{3}{2}}$

   (4) $(6.5 + \frac{3}{2})(40 + 6)$

   (5) $(6.5 - \frac{3}{2})(40 + 6)$

ANSWERS ARE ON PAGE 90.

39. As shown at right, which of the following conditions is (are) sufficient to ensure that △*ABC* is an isosceles triangle?

A. ∠*B* = 90°
B. ∠*B* = 110°
C. side *BC* = 15 inches

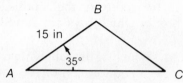

(1) A only   **(2)** B only   **(3)** C only   **(4)** A or B   **(5)** B or C

40. As shown below, the support poles of a swing make an angle of 48° with each other. What is the value, in degrees, of the acute angle that each post makes with the ground?

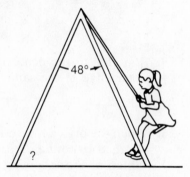

(1) 46°
(2) 58°
(3) 66°
(4) 72°
(5) Not enough information is given.

41. As part of a school contest, each student receives 5 points for each book he or she reads at home, 2 points for each report he or she gives in class on current events, and 2 points for each special project. Which expression tells how many points Alex earned during a month in which he read 4 books, gave 3 class reports, and completed 1 special project?

(1) 5(4) + 2(3 + 1)   **(4)** (5 + 2) + (4 + 3 + 1)
(2) 5(3) + 2(4 + 1)   **(5)** (5 + 2)(4 + 3 + 1)
(3) (5)(2) + (4 + 3 + 1)

42. Janice wants to buy 3 pounds of oranges and 6 pounds of chicken. According to the advertised sale prices, in which of the following stores can she get the best buy?

John's Market: Oranges for $.85 per pound, and chicken for $1.30 per pound. John's is giving an additional 5% discount for all purchases over $5.00.

Shopper's Market: Oranges for $.90 per pound, and chicken for $1.25 per pound.

Best Buy Groceries: Oranges for $.95 per pound, and chicken for $1.20 per pound. Best Buy is giving an additional 10% discount on all sales over $20.00.

Food Plus: Oranges for $.80 per pound, and chicken for $1.20 per pound.

(1) John's Market
(2) Shopper's Market
(3) Best Buy Groceries
(4) Food Plus
(5) either Shopper's Market or Food Plus

ANSWERS ARE ON PAGE 90.

43. Rob bought four boxes of bolts, the sizes of which are listed below. He wants to place the longest bolts in the left-hand drawer of his utility cabinet, the next longest in the next drawer, and so on.

Box A: $\frac{25}{32}$-inch bolts

Box B: $\frac{5}{8}$-inch bolts

Box C: $\frac{13}{16}$-inch bolts

Box D: $\frac{3}{4}$-inch bolts

Listing the longest bolt first, which sequence correctly lists the order in which the drawers should be filled from left to right?

(1) B, C, A, D

(2) C, A, D, B

(3) A, B, D, C

(4) C, A, B, D

(5) B, C, D, A

44. James sells used appliances. Last week he sold 5 appliances from his "Under $200" room, and he sold several higher-priced used appliances as indicated at right.

Number Sold	Price
3	$299
4	$349
2	$389

What additional information is needed in order to determine the average price of the appliances that James sold last week?

(1) the number of appliances he sold for under $200

(2) the lowest price received for an appliance under $200

(3) the median price received for an appliance under $200

(4) the average price received for an appliance under $200

(5) the highest price received for an appliance under $200

45. Which expression has the same value as $x^3 + 4x^2$?

(1) $3x(x + 8)$

(2) $4x^2(x + 1)$

(3) $x^2(x + 4x^2)$

(4) $(x + 4)(x + 4)$

(5) $x^2(x + 4)$

46. Which of the following most nearly equals, in feet, the length of a side of a square that has an area of 180 square feet?

(1) $3\sqrt{7}$ **(2)** $4\sqrt{6}$ **(3)** $6\sqrt{5}$ **(4)** $5\sqrt{6}$ **(5)** $8\sqrt{2}$

Questions 47–48 refer to the following graph.

47. As shown on the graph, the line $y = -2x + 4$ passes through the points (1,2) and (2,0). What are the x |=| and y |=| intercepts of this line?

(1) x-intercept = −2 y-intercept = 4

(2) x-intercept = 1 y-intercept = 2

(3) x-intercept = 2 y-intercept = 0

(4) x-intercept = 2 y-intercept = 2

(5) x-intercept = 2 y-intercept = 4

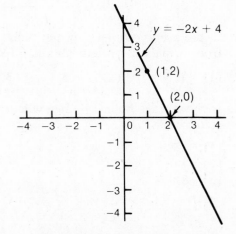

ANSWERS ARE ON PAGE 90.

48. What is the slope of the line $y = -2x + 4$?

    (1) −2   **(2)** −1   **(3)** 1   **(4)** 2   **(5)** 4

49. What are the two solutions to the quadratic equation $x^2 + 4x - 12 = 0$?

    (1) $x = 2, x = 6$ **(4)** $x = 3, x = 4$
    (2) $x = -2, x = 6$ **(5)** $x = 3, x = -4$
    (3) $x = 2, x = -6$

50. On a hiking trip on the trails shown at right, Kathy walked 12 miles north of the campsite and then took a second trail for 5 miles directly east. What is the direct distance, in miles, from Kathy's position to the campsite?

    (1) 7
    (2) 10
    (3) 12
    (4) 13
    (5) 15

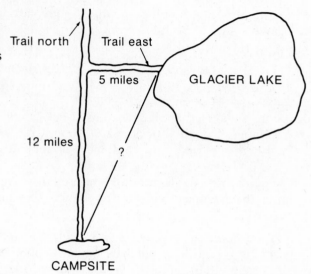

Questions 51–52 refer to the following illustration.

SOURCES OF PROTEIN IN AMERICAN DIET
(Percent obtained from major food groups)

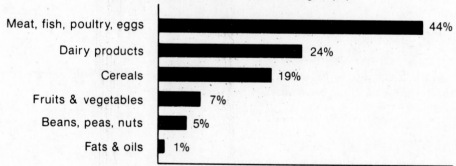

51. In the average American diet, what is the approximate ratio of protein obtained from cereals to protein obtained from dairy products?

    (1) 3 to 5   **(2)** 2 to 3   **(3)** 2 to 5   **(4)** 4 to 5   **(5)** 4 to 7

52. In the average American diet, what percent of total calories is obtained from protein sources?

    (1) 32%   **(4)** 100%
    (2) 44%   **(5)** Not enough information is given.
    (3) 68%

ANSWERS ARE ON PAGE 91.

53. Loaded with 12 new cars, Martin's truck and trailer have a total weight of 4.5×10^4 pounds. For safe passage over older bridges, state engineers have set a weight limit of 1.35×10^5 pounds for truck/trailers the size of Martin's. Considering this weight limit, which of the following is true about Martin's loaded truck and trailer?

Martin's truck and trailer weigh approximately:
(1) twice as much as the maximum allowable weight
(2) three times as much as the maximum allowable weight
(3) one-half the maximum allowable weight
(4) one-third the maximum allowable weight
(5) one-thirtieth the maximum allowable weight

54. The following stores are offering sale prices on apples:

At Amy's Market, apples are on sale for $4.00 per dozen.
At Friendly Shopper, apples are on sale for $.69 per pound.
At Super Savers, apples are on sale for $5.00 per bagful.

To determine which store is offering the lowest price per pound, which additional information do you need?

A. the average weight of apples at Amy's Market
B. the average number of apples in a bagful at Super Savers
C. the average weight of a bagful of apples at Super Savers

(1) A only   **(4)** A and B only
(2) B only   **(5)** A and C only
(3) C only

55. Betty, Lynn, and Rhonda are having lunch together. Betty's meal costs $.75 less than Lynn's. Rhonda's meal costs $.45 more than Lynn's. If the total bill plus tax comes to $12.90, what is the cost of Betty's meal?

(1) $3.11   **(4)** $5.15
(2) $3.65   **(5)** Not enough information is given.
(3) $4.40

56. The triangle in the drawing at right has the same area as the rectangle beside it. Using the dimensions given in the drawing, determine the height, in feet, of the triangle.

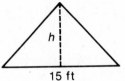 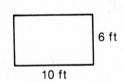

(1) 6
(2) 8
(3) 10
(4) 12
(5) 14

ANSWERS ARE ON PAGE 91.

Practice Test Answer Key

1. (2) 2.2 cm
The distance separating points A and B is the difference in their readings.

Point B = 4.0 cm
Point A = 1.8 cm

$$\begin{array}{r} 4.0 \\ -\ 1.8 \\ \hline \end{array}$$

Difference   2.2

2. (5) five subtracted from three times a number
$3x$ is read "three times a number".
In $3x - 5$, 5 is subtracted from $3x$.

3. (3) 10 × 1
Round each amount to the nearest whole number.

9 pounds 15 ounces ≅ 10 pounds
$1.02 ≅ $1.00.
10 × 1 is the approximate price in dollars.

4. (4) 23 gallons 1 quart
Quarts per month = 3 × 31 = 93

Gallons per month = $\frac{93}{4}$

$\qquad = 23\frac{1}{4}$ gallons

$\qquad = 23$ gallons 1 quart

5. (2) x^3y
When dividing, subtract the exponents of like variables.

$$\frac{x^5y^3}{x^2y^2} = x^{5-2}y^{3-2} = x^3y$$

6. (4) 43°F
To determine how much colder −53°F is than −10°F, subtract −53 from −10.

$$-10 - (-53) = -10 + 53 = 43$$

7. (1) $525
Savings = principal + interest
$\qquad = \$500 + prt$
$\qquad = \$500 + (\$500)(.025)(2)$
$\qquad = \$500 + \$25$
$\qquad = \$525$

8. (3) $471
Down payment = $79
Total monthly payments = $49 × 8 = $392
Total cost to Harriet = $79 + $392 = $471
The sale price, $439, is not relevant.

9. (3) $\dfrac{120}{(168 + 120)}$
Distance from Walterville to Woodland
$\qquad = 120$
Distance from Walterville to Rosa Bay
$\qquad = 168 + 120$

Expressed as a fraction of the total, Woodland is $\frac{120}{(168 + 120)}$ of the way from Walterville to Rosa Bay.

10. (2) $321
One way to solve this problem is to add the fractions first.

$$\frac{1}{6} + \frac{1}{4} + \frac{1}{3} = \frac{9}{12} = \frac{3}{4}$$

If $\frac{3}{4}$ is spent, $\frac{1}{4}$ remains.

$$\frac{1}{4} \times \$1284 = \$321$$

11. (3) 3.3 miles
Compute the distance around the bike path.

one lap = $2\pi r = 2 \times \frac{22}{7} \times 154$
$\qquad = 968$ yards

Six laps is 6 × 968 = 5,808 yards
To change yards to miles, divide by 1,760.

$$\frac{5,808}{1,760} = 3.3 \text{ miles}$$

12. (4) 7
Determine the length of ribbon to be divided.

$$25 - 8\frac{1}{2} = 16\frac{1}{2} \text{ feet}$$

Divide this piece by $2\frac{1}{4}$.

$$16\frac{1}{2} - 2\frac{1}{4} = 7\frac{1}{3}$$

Sally was able to cut 7 pieces. The leftover piece is not counted.

13. (3) 40
When you know the percent and the part, divide the part by the percent to find the whole. Write 35% as .35.

$$\frac{14}{.35} = 40$$

14. (3) 1980
Sales of $1,000,000 occur only when five or more $200,000 symbols appear next to the year. The first time this occurs is in 1980 (six symbols).

15. (1) $950,000
One way to solve the problem is to find the average number of symbols per year during the first four years reported.

Total number of symbols first four years
$\qquad = 19$
Average number per year
$\qquad = \frac{19}{4}$
$\qquad = 4.75$

To change symbols to dollars, multiply by $200,000.
4.75 × $200,000 = $950,000

16. (2) $1,300,000
Because there are 6 years reported, the median is the average of the two middle values:
1980 value = 6 × $200,000 = $1,200,000
1985 value = 7 × $200,000 = $1,400,000
Average of 1980 and 1985 values
$\qquad = \$1,300,000$

17. (3) 0
Solve the inequality for x by adding 1 to each term: $-2 < x < 1$
The only listed value of x that is larger than -2 but less than 1 is 0.
$$-2 < 0 < 1$$

18. (1) \$375
$i = prt$
where $p = \$2,500$, $r = 18\% = \frac{18}{100}$,
$$t = \frac{10}{12} = \frac{5}{6}$$
$$i = (\$2,500)\left(\frac{18}{100}\right)\left(\frac{5}{6}\right)$$
$$= (\$2,500)\left(\frac{3}{20}\right)$$
$$= \$375$$

19. (2) $\frac{1}{3}$
There are 9 pairs of socks in Henry's drawer, 3 of which are dark blue. The probability of picking dark blue on the first try is therefore $\frac{3}{9} = \frac{1}{3}$.

20. (2) $\frac{1}{2}$
Morning distance $= 2 \times 45 = 90$ miles
Afternoon distance $= 3 \times 60 = 180$ miles
$$\frac{\text{Morning distance}}{\text{Afternoon distance}} = \frac{90}{180} = \frac{1}{2}$$

21. (1) 28°
The ladder, house, and ground form a triangle. The three angles of the triangle must add up to 180°.

Ladder-ground angle $= 62°$
House-ground angle $= 90°$
Ladder-house angle $= 180° - (90° + 62°)$
$\qquad\qquad\qquad\quad = 180° - 152°$
$\qquad\qquad\qquad\quad = 28°$

22. (4) 52
$$\text{Average Speed } = \frac{\text{distance}}{\text{time}}$$
$$= \frac{338}{6.5} \text{ since 30 minutes is .5 hours}$$
$$= 52 \text{ miles per hour}$$

23. (3) 9
Kyle's team won 3 out of each 5 games they played. They therefore won $\frac{3}{5}$ of their games.
$$\tfrac{3}{5} \text{ of } 15 = \tfrac{3}{5} \times 15 = 9$$

24. (4) 40%
Percent increase = amount of increase divided by original amount
Amount of increase $= \$6.30 - \$4.50 = \$1.80$
Percent increase $= \frac{1.80}{4.50} = .4 = 40\%$

25. (4) 130°
$$\angle A + 50° = 180°$$
$$\angle A = 180° - 50°$$
$$\angle A = 130°$$

26. (3) 392
Size of backyard $= 28 \times 20 = 560$ square yards
Amount of garden space
$$= (\tfrac{1}{2})(12)(28)$$
$$= 168 \text{ square yards}$$
Square yards of grass
$$= 560 - 168$$
$$= 392 \text{ square yards}$$

27. (5) \$1110
Cash needed when Kramers move in.
First month's rent: \$430
Cleaning deposit: 280
Security deposit: 400
Total: \$1110

28. (3) \$3.40
Total of deposits $= \$280 + \$400 = \$680$
$$i = prt$$
$$= (\$680)\left(\frac{6}{100}\right)\left(\frac{1}{12}\right)$$
$$= \$3.40$$

29. (5) Not enough information is given.
The owner will require the Kramers to pay the entire cost of repairing the door. Part of this cost is the bill of the repairman—an amount that is not given in the problem.

30. (5) $65t = 2840$
Let t = time Jill types
$65t$ = number of words Jill can type in time t

For Jill to finish the report in time t, $65t$ must equal the number of words in the report.
$$65t = 2840$$

31. (4) 91
Sales before price reduction $= 70$
Sales after price reduction $= 70 + 30\%$ of 70
$\qquad\qquad\qquad\qquad\qquad = 70 + .3 \times 70$
$\qquad\qquad\qquad\qquad\qquad = 70 + 21$
$\qquad\qquad\qquad\qquad\qquad = 91$

32. (5) 27
Let h equal unknown height of sail on model. Write a proportion of two equal ratios:
$$\frac{\text{height}}{\text{width}} = \frac{h}{12} = \frac{18}{8}$$
Solve for h: $h = \frac{18}{8}(12) = \frac{54}{2} = 27$

33. (2) 168
Out of every 11 cartons of milk that are drunk, 7 are regular and 4 are chocolate. Therefore $\frac{4}{11}$ of all cartons are chocolate.
$$\tfrac{4}{11} \text{ of } 462 = \tfrac{4}{11} \times 462$$
$$= 168$$

34. (3) $\pi 8^2 - 3^2$

The area of the sandy part is equal to the total area subtract the area of the toy box. Total area of sand box including the toy box

$$= \pi 8^2$$

Total area of toy box

$$= 3^2$$

Area of sandy part $= \pi 8^2 - 3^2$

35. (2) 50

The distance around the outer edge is equal to the circumference of a circle with a radius of 8 feet.

$$\text{distance} = 2\pi r = (2)(3.14)(8)$$
$$= 50.24 \cong 50 \text{ feet}$$

36. (4) $10 - 16(.17) - 4(.79)$

The change Russ should receive is equal to $10 minus the cost of each of his purchases.

$$\text{cost of watermelon} = 16(\$.17)$$
$$\text{cost of cherries} = 4(\$.79)$$

Amount of change $= \$10 - 16(\$.17) - 4(\$.79)$

37. (4) 8

Area of lower part of patio $= 5 \times 8$
$$= 40 \text{ square yards}$$
Area of upper part of patio $= 4 \times 2$
$$= 8 \text{ square yards}$$
Total area of patio
$$= 40 + 8 = 48 \text{ square yards}$$
The volume of the patio is equal to its area times its thickness: 6 inches $= \frac{1}{6}$ yard
$$\text{Volume} = 48 \times \frac{1}{6} = 8 \text{ cubic yards}$$

38. (2) $40(6.5) + 6(\frac{3}{2})(6.5)$

Total earnings $=$ regular $+$ overtime
Regular weekly earnings $= 40(6.5)$

Overtime weekly earnings $= 6(\frac{3}{2})(6.5)$

Total earnings $= 40(6.5) + 6(\frac{3}{2})(6.5)$

39. (5) B or C

Triangle ABC wil be an isosceles triangle if side BC is also equal to 15 in, or if $\angle C$ is also equal to 35°. If $\angle B = 110°$, then $\angle C$ is equal to 35°.

$(\angle C = 180° - 110° - 35° = 35°)$

Therefore, either condition B or C ensures that triangle ABC is isosceles.

40. (3) 66°

The sum of the three angles inside the triangle equals 180°. Since the two unknown angles are equal, the sum of these two angles is equal to $180° - 48° = 132°$. Therefore, each unknown angle is equal to $\frac{132°}{2} = 66°$.

41. (1) $5(4) + 2(3 + 1)$

Alex got the following points:
4 books $= 5(4)$
3 reports $= 2(3)$
1 project $= 2(1)$
Total points $= 5(4) + 2(3) + 2(1)$
$$= 5(4) + 2(3 + 1)$$
since $2(3 + 1) = 2(3) + 2(1)$

42. (4) Food Plus

The total price that Janice would pay in each store is listed below.
 John's Market: $9.83 (rounded to nearest cent after discount)
 Shopper's Market: $10.20
 Best Buy Groceries: $10.05
 Food Plus: $9.60

43. (2) C, A, D, B

For purposes of comparison, change each length to 32s of an inch.

Box A: $= \frac{25}{32}$

Box B: $= \frac{20}{32}$

Box C: $= \frac{26}{32}$

Box D: $= \frac{24}{32}$

From longest to shortest, the order is C, A, D, B

44. (4) the average price received for an appliance under $200

To determine this average, you need to know the total money James made from all appliance sales. The only missing information is the total amount received from the low-cost appliances. You can determine this amount, though, if you know the number of low-priced appliances sold (5) and know their average cost.

45. (5) $x^2(x + 4)$

x can be factored out of each term in the expression $x^3 + 4x^2$. Or, you can multiply each answer choice out and see that (5) is correct.

46. (3) $6\sqrt{5}$

Let $s =$ side of the square
$$s^2 = \text{area of square}$$
$$s^2 = 180$$
$$s = \sqrt{180}$$
$$= \sqrt{36 \cdot 5} = \sqrt{36}\sqrt{5}$$
$$= 6\sqrt{5}$$

47. (5) x intercept $= 2$ y intercept $= 4$

The x intercept is $x = 2$, the point where the line crosses the x axis. The y intercept is $y = 4$, the point where the line crosses the y axis.

48. (1) −2
The slope can most easily be found using the two intercepts.

$$\frac{\text{change in } y \text{ value}}{\text{change in } x \text{ value}} = \frac{4 - 0}{0 - 2} = \frac{4}{-2} = -2$$

49. (3) $x = 2, x = -6$
Trying each pair of x values, you find that only $x = 2$ and $x = -6$ solve the equation: $x^2 + 4x - 12$.

$x = 2$
$2^2 + 4 \cdot 2 - 12 = 4 + 8 - 12 = 0$

$x = -6$
$(-6)^2 + 4(-6) - 12 = 36 - 24 - 12 = 0$

50. (4) 13
Let d = the unknown distance
According to the Pythagorean Theorem:
$$d^2 = 12^2 + 5^2$$
$$= 144 + 25 \quad \text{Check:} \quad 13$$
$$d^2 = 169 \qquad\qquad \times 13$$
$$\text{or, } d = 13 \qquad\qquad \overline{169}$$

51. (4) 4 to 5
Protein obtained from cereals = 19%
Protein obtained from dairy products = 24%
Ratio = 19 to 24 ≅ 4 to 5

Check $\frac{19}{24} \cong .792$

$\frac{4}{5} = .8$

$\frac{3}{4} = .75$

$\frac{5}{6} \cong .83$

52. (5) Not enough information is given.
No information is given about what percent of total calories is obtained from protein sources. The graph deals only with a breakdown of protein sources themselves.

53. (4) one-third the maximum allowable weight
Writing whole numbers, the maximum weight limit is 135,000 pounds. Martin's loaded rig weighs 45,000 pounds. Martin's rig weighs $\frac{1}{3}$ of the weight limit.

54. (5) A and C only
To determine weight per pound, you need to be able to compute the weight per pound at each store, regardless of whether the store sells apples by the dozen, or by the bagful. Choice A enables you to determine weight per pound at Amy's market, and choice C enables you to determine weight per pound at Super Savers. Choice B is of no help.

55. (2) $3.65
Let x = cost of Lynn's meal
$x - .75$ = cost of Betty's meal
$x + .45$ = cost of Rhonda's meal

Set the sum = 12.90, the amount of bill
$$x + x - .75 + x + .45 = 12.90$$
$$3x - .30 = 12.90$$
$$3x = 13.20$$
$$x = 4.40$$
$$x - .75 = 3.65$$

56. (2) 8
Let h = height of triangle

Area of triangle = $\frac{1}{2} \cdot 15 \cdot h$

Area of rectangle = $10 \cdot 6 = 60$

$$\frac{1}{2} \cdot 15 \cdot h = 60$$
$$15 \cdot h = 120$$
$$h = \frac{120}{15} = 8$$

Practice Test Evaluation Chart

This chart will help you determine the areas in which you may need review work. Circle the numbers of any items you got wrong, then fill in the number correct for each skill area. Below you will find review page references for both this exercise book and Contemporary's *GED Mathematics Test* satellite text.

Skill Area	Item Numbers	Satellite Review Pages	Exercise Book Review Pages	Number Correct
Problem Solving with Whole Numbers	8, 27, 29, 36, 38, 41, 44	21–51	8–17	_____/7
Decimals	42	53–77	18–23	_____/1
Fractions	9, 10	79–115	24–29	_____/2
Probability, Ratio, and Proportion	19, 20, 23, 33	117–129	30–34	_____/4
Percents	7, 13, 18, 24, 28, 31	131–163	35–39	_____/6
Measurement	1, 3, 4, 12, 43, 54	165–175	40–45	_____/6
Graphs and Tables	14, 15, 16, 51, 52	177–193	46–55	_____/5
Basics of Algebra	2, 22, 30, 55	195–221	56–61	_____/4
Geometry	11, 21, 25, 26, 32, 34, 35, 37, 39, 40, 50, 56	223–277	62–71	_____/12
Special Topics in Algebra and Geometry	5, 6, 17, 45, 46, 47, 48, 49, 53	279–313	72–77	_____/9
			Total	_____/56

Answer Key

PROBLEM SOLVING WITH WHOLE NUMBERS

A 5-Step Approach to Problem Solving
pages 8-9

1. 21 lb
2. $6900
3. 288 cars
4. 7 lb
5. 15 oil changes
6. $6.49
7. $12.13
8. $46.00
9. 41,400 mi
10. (4) $17.84
11. (2) 20 teachers
12. (4) $33.84
13. (5) 312 cans
14. (1) $575

Insufficient Information
pages 10-11

1. the amount of time Brenda practices each Tuesday and Thursday
2. the number of boys in the class
3. the amount of tips Carol received
4. the number of months payments are to be made
5. the amount of time he stopped for lunch
6. the sale price of the salmon steak
7. the number of calories in a glass of milk
8. the number of friends with Carlin

Mean, Median, and Number Series
pages 12-13

1. 11 lb
2. $10/hr
3. 49
4. 134
5. $192.44
6. 7:00 A.M.
7. 7 absences
8. 12 points above passing
9. 1330 mi
10. $41
11. 92°F
12. 11 yr
13. 130
14. (4) add 6, subtract 3
15. 32
16. 130
17. 10
18. $701
19. 20 lb
20. 12:20 P.M.

Set-up Questions
pages 14-16

1. **(1) 12 + 15**
   To remove parentheses, multiply each of the numbers 4 and 5 by 3.
   $(3)(4 + 5) = (3)(4) + (3)(5)$
   $= 12 + 15$

2. **(4) 160 − 2**
   In the expression $(20)(8) - \frac{6}{3}$, 20 multiplies only the 8.
   $(20)(8) - \frac{6}{3} = 160 - \frac{6}{3}$
   $= 160 - 2$

3. **(2) (8)(7) − (8)(4)**
   To remove parentheses, multiply each of the numbers 7 and 4 by 8. The product (8)(4) is subtracted from the product (8)(7).
   $(8)(7 - 4) = (8)(7) - (8)(4)$

4. **(5) (5)(2 + 6)**
   The expression (5)(2) + (5)(6) has the same value as the expression (5)(2 + 6). This can be checked by multiplying the second expression.
   $(5)(2 + 6) = (5)(2) + (5)(6)$

5. **(3) (189)(250 + 82)**
   The dollar amount of sales can be written as the price of the lawnmower ($189) times the total number of lawnmowers sold (250 + 82).
   ($189)(250 + 82)

6. **(1) (5)(3) + (4)(2)**
   Shellie works 5 hours per day on each of 3 days, for a total of (5)(3) hours. She also works 4 hours per day on each of 2 days for a total of (4)(2) hours. Altogether she works (5)(3) + (4)(2) hours.

7. **(5) (4)(46 + 41)**
   Working together, Mickey and Elvin can lay (46 + 41) floor tiles in 1 hour. In 4 hours they can lay 4 times this many: (4)(46 + 41)

8. **(3) 1325 − (245 + 68 + 42)**
   Floyd's take-home pay after taxes can be represented as his gross pay minus the sum of the three deductions.
   $1325 − ($245 + $68 + $42)

9. **(4) $\frac{(150 + 162 + 148)}{3}$**
   To compute the average for the first 3 months, add only the gallons used during those months. Then, divide this sum by 3:
   $$\frac{(150 + 162 + 148)}{3}$$
   Information concerning the final 2 months is not relevant.

10. (4) $\dfrac{(230)(640)}{54}$

Total time it will take Carmen = the total number of words in the manuscript divided by the rate at which Carmen types.
Total number of words in manuscript = (230)(640)
Total time needed = $\dfrac{(230)(640)}{54}$

11. (2) $\dfrac{(60-42)}{50}$

To determine the amount of dough in each turnover, divide the amount of dough left over by 50.
Amount of dough left over = 60 − 42
Amount of dough in each turnover = $\dfrac{(60-42)}{50}$

12. (4) $\dfrac{(130-2)}{8}+2$

Each child in the class was given $\dfrac{(130-2)}{8}$ crayons. Sally was given 2 extra crayons: $\dfrac{(130-2)}{8}+2$

Item Sets
pages 16–17

1. 59 gal
2. 1737 mi

3. **(5) Not enough information is given.**
The passage does not tell us how many miles Gloria drove on each of the 3rd, 4th, and 5th days of her trips. We are told only the total of these three days.

4. **(3) 402**
During the first 2 days of her trip, Gloria drove 440 + 364 = 804 miles. She drove 804 more miles on the last two days of her trip. During these four days she drove 804 + 804 = 1608 miles. Dividing 1608 by 4 gives her average mileage per day during these 4 days.
$\frac{1608}{4}$ = 402

5. **$5.78**
6. **$.74**

7. **(2) $.88**
Cost at Burger Palace of 2 children's meals: 2 × $2.45 = $4.90
Cost at Happy Mealtime of 2 children's meals:
2($1.25 + $.89 + $.75) = 2($2.89) = $5.78
Difference in price: $5.78 − $4.90 = $.88

8. **(5) Not enough information is given.**
The passage does not give the individual prices of burgers and fries at Burger Palace. You can assume the price would be less than $2.45 per child, but you don't know how much less.

9. **543 mi**
10. **364 mi**
11. **(5) 182**
Looking at the map, you see that the shortest route from Wilsonville to Fall River is also the shortest route from Wilsonville to Loveland. You can determine the distance along each route from Wilsonville to Loveland without knowing the distance from Loveland to Fall River.

DECIMALS
Part One
pages 18–19

1. .3	16. $.79
2. .38	17. 25.3 miles per gallon
3. three	
4. five and one hundred thirty-four thousandths	18. 15.18 thousand square miles
	19. 17.7 MHz
5. .0423, .4023, 4.023, 40.23	20. .250
6. 18.024	21. .125 in
7. 7.16	22. 2.06 m
8. $4.11	23. .664 in
9. 2.133	24. $200.55
10. 4.86	25. 42 lb
11. 6.18	26. $30.24
12. 11.05	27. $3.85
13. 1.88	28. $4.63
14. 410	29. 24 mi
15. $41.83	30. .14 kg

Part Two
pages 20–21

1. 8.825 lb
2. 17.8 lb
3. 16.01 million dollars
4. 44.83 g
5. (4) 3.9 mi
6. (4) $64.19
7. (3) $21.49
8. (5) Not enough information is given.
9. (4) 2.5 cm
10. (1) $1.06

Part Three
pages 21–23

1. **(3) 56.3**
To compute the average, add the scores and divide by 3.

$56\frac{1}{3}$ = 56.33...
$3\overline{)169}$ since $\frac{1}{3}$ = .33...

57
49
+ 63
169

15
19
18
1

2. (5) 53.333333
Divide 160 by 3, and keep only the first 8 digits.

$$53\tfrac{1}{3} = 53.333333\ldots$$
$$3\overline{)160}$$
$$\underline{15} \quad \text{since } \tfrac{1}{3} = .33\ldots$$
$$10$$
$$\underline{9}$$
$$1$$

3. (3) $6.95
The minimum cost would be to rent a bike for the 4-hour rate and for 2 additional hours at the hourly rate.
2 hours at the hourly rate = $2.70
4 hours at the 4-hour rate = $\underline{\$4.25}$
Total rental price = $6.95

4. (2) 2(24.65) + 3($29.95)
The cost of 2 Grade B sheets is 2($24.65)
The cost of 3 Grade A sheets is 3($29.95)
The total price is found by adding these two costs: 2($24.65) + 3($29.95)

5. (4) .875 inch
Total thickness of 4 washers = .0625 × 4
= .25 inch
Amount of bolt uncovered = 1.125 − .25
= .875 inch

6. (2) $\dfrac{(6 - 2.8)}{6}$
To determine the length of pipe to be divided, subtract:
(6 − 2.8) meters
Divide this piece by 6.
$\dfrac{(6 - 2.8)}{6}$ meters

7. (5) A or C
To determine the average length, you must know the exact length of each bolt. Since you know the size differences, you can determine the exact lengths of all the bolts if you know the exact length of any one of them. Either choice A or choice C gives the needed information.

8. (4) 8
Compute the amount of space taken up by the 64 books: 64 × 1.2 = 76.8 inches. The left over space is 94 − 76.8 = 17.2 inches.
To determine how many 2-inch wide books will fit, divide 17.2 by 2 and drop any remainder:
$\dfrac{17.2}{2}$ = 8.6. Answer: 8 2-inch wide books

9. (2) 103.1
To find the average, add the five temperatures, and divide the sum by 5.

104.7°F
103.9°F $\dfrac{515.7}{5} = 103.14 \cong 103.1$
102.8°F
102.4°F
$\underline{101.9°F}$
515.7°F

10. (1) B, C, D, A
Give all 4 weights the same number of decimal places and compare the numbers.
Load A = .629 ton
Load B = .714 ton
Load C = .709 ton
Load D = .680 ton
From heaviest to lightest, the correct order is .714, .709, .680, .629 = B, C, D, A

11. (4) $235.40
To compute the cost, multiply the number of kilowatt-hours times the rate.
2750 × $.0856 = $235.40

12. (3) $.0116
Rate this December: $.0856
Rate last December: $\underline{\$.074}$
Difference: $.0116

13. (2) 2835
To find the total power used, divide the electric bill by the rate.
$\dfrac{\$209.79}{\$.074}$ = 2835 kilowatt-hours

FRACTIONS
Part One
pages 24–25

1. $\tfrac{2}{5}$
2. $4\tfrac{2}{3}$
3. $2\tfrac{1}{2}$
4. 7
5. $4\tfrac{2}{5}$
6. $7\tfrac{5}{24}$
7. $\tfrac{15}{24}$
8. $\tfrac{31}{8}$
9. $26\tfrac{1}{4}$
10. $14\tfrac{2}{3}$
11. $2\tfrac{1}{2}$
12. $\tfrac{33}{52}$
13. $\tfrac{3}{8}$

14. .24
15. $\tfrac{4}{9}$
16. $\tfrac{2}{5}$
17. $\tfrac{3}{5}$
18. $10\tfrac{3}{8}$ in
19. $\tfrac{5}{16}$
20. $7\tfrac{5}{6}$ yd
21. $\tfrac{15}{16}$ in
22. 49 homes
23. $22\tfrac{1}{2}$ gal
24. $\tfrac{3}{8}$
25. $\tfrac{4}{7}$

Part Two
pages 25–26

1. $19\frac{5}{8}$ in
2. $13\frac{5}{8}$ mi
3. $\frac{3}{4}$
4. $\frac{17}{40}$
5. $\frac{7}{16}$ in
6. 10 boys
7. (1) $3\frac{1}{4}$ ft

8. (5) Not enough information is given.
9. (2) $4.84
10. (2) $\frac{11}{16}$ lb
11. (5) Not enough information is given.
12. $\frac{19}{55}$

Part Three
pages 27–29

1. **(3) 29**
   Add the three salad weights. Divide this sum by $\frac{5}{8}$.
   $$8\frac{1}{4} + 6\frac{1}{4} + 3\frac{5}{8} = 17\frac{9}{8} = 18\frac{1}{8}$$
   $$18\frac{1}{8} \div \frac{5}{8} = 29$$

2. **(5) $16\frac{1}{8}$**
   By subtracting you find that between each two dates shown Bea lost $5\frac{3}{8}$ pounds. Following the same pattern, Bea will lose $3 \times 5\frac{3}{8}$ more pounds in the next 3 months.
   $$163\frac{7}{8} - 158\frac{1}{2} = 5\frac{3}{8}$$
   $$5\frac{3}{8} \times 3 = \frac{129}{8} = 16\frac{1}{8}$$

3. **(2) $\frac{9}{16}$**
   Subtract Wednesday's reading from Thursday's.
   $$1\frac{3}{16} - \frac{5}{8} = \frac{9}{16}$$

4. **(2) $1\frac{9}{32}$**
   To determine the record, add $\frac{3}{32}$ to $1\frac{3}{16}$.
   $$1\frac{3}{16} + \frac{3}{32} = 1\frac{9}{32}$$

5. **(4) $3\frac{3}{4}$**
   Add the five amounts shown.
   $$\frac{5}{16} + \frac{3}{8} + \frac{5}{8} + 1\frac{3}{16} + 1\frac{1}{4} = 2\frac{28}{16} = 3\frac{3}{4}$$

6. **(3) $\frac{3}{4}$ inch**
   Add the five amounts shown and divide the sum by 5. From Problem #9, the sum is $3\frac{3}{4}$ inches.
   $$3\frac{3}{4} \div 5 = \frac{3}{4}$$

7. **(5) $(\frac{5}{2})(1.09) + (\frac{13}{4})(2.84)$**
   Wei-Chuan paid $(2\frac{1}{2})(1.09)$ for the chicken and $(3\frac{1}{4})(2.84)$ for the cheese. Expressing each mixed number as an improper fraction and adding, you get answer choice (5).
   $$(2\frac{1}{2})(1.09) = (\frac{5}{2})(1.09)$$
   $$(3\frac{1}{4})(2.84) = (\frac{13}{4})(2.84)$$

8. **(1) $\frac{1}{6}$**
   To find the difference in price reductions between clothing items and hardware items, subtract $\frac{1}{3}$ from $\frac{1}{2}$.
   $$\frac{1}{2} - \frac{1}{3} = \frac{1}{6}$$

9. **(4) a hand saw originally selling for $13.48**
   Compute the amount saved on each item. The answer is the item with the largest discount.
   hammer: $\frac{1}{2}$ of $12.50 is $6.25
   frying pan: $\frac{1}{4}$ of $22.88 is $5.72
   pants: $\frac{1}{3}$ of $18.99 is $6.33
   saw: $\frac{1}{2}$ of $13.48 is $6.74
   dress: $\frac{1}{3}$ of $19.59 is $6.53

10. **(3) $\frac{13}{36}$**
    Add the three price reduction fractions and divide the sum by 3.
    $$\frac{1}{2} + \frac{1}{3} + \frac{1}{4} = \frac{13}{12}$$
    $$\frac{13}{12} \div 3 = \frac{13}{36}$$

11. **(4) $50 - (\frac{1}{2})(18) - (\frac{2}{3})(23)$**
    Flo will pay $\frac{1}{2}$ of $18 for the shovel. She will save $\frac{1}{3}$ on the price of the blouse; therefore she will pay $\frac{2}{3}$ of $23, the original price of the blouse. Her change will be 50 subtract each of the two amounts she pays.
    $$50 - (\frac{1}{2})(18) - (\frac{2}{3})(23)$$

12. **(1) C, A, B, D**
    For purposes of comparison, write each weight as a mixed decimal.
    Gravel A = 1.6 tons
    Gravel B = 1.59 tons
    Gravel C = 1.625 tons
    Gravel D = 1.5625 tons
    From heaviest to lightest, the order is C, A, B, D

13. **(2) $\frac{3}{20}$**
    Out of a gross amount of $15,000, $2,250 is withheld for federal taxes. As a fraction, $\frac{2250}{15,000}$ is withheld for federal taxes.
    $$\frac{2250 \div 10}{15,000 \div 10} = \frac{225}{1500}; \quad \frac{225 \div 25}{1500 \div 25} = \frac{9}{60} = \frac{3}{20}$$

14. (1) $\frac{1}{15}$

Out of a gross amount of $15,000, approximately $1000 is withheld for social security. As a fraction, $\frac{1000}{15,000}$ is withheld for social security.

$$\frac{1000 \div 1000}{15,000 \div 1000} = \frac{1}{15}$$

15. (5) $\frac{1}{3}$

The fraction formed by dividing the amount withheld for state taxes ($740) by the amount withheld for federal taxes ($2250) is $\frac{740}{2250}$. Of the answer choices given, $\frac{740}{2250}$ is closest to $\frac{1}{3}$.

Check: $740 \times 3 = 2220$

$740 \times 4 = 2960$

16. (3) $3,000

Kenneth's federal taxes will increase by $\frac{1}{3}$ of their present amount.
$\frac{1}{3}$ of $2250 is $750.
$2250 + $750 = $3000

PROBABILITY, RATIO, AND PROPORTION

Part One
pages 30–31

1. $\frac{1}{7}$

2. $\frac{3}{7}$

3. $\frac{4}{7}$

4. $\frac{2}{5}$

5. $\frac{1}{3}$

6. $\frac{3}{14}$

7. $\frac{1}{35}$

8. 2:3 or $\frac{2}{3}$

9. 7:6 or $\frac{7}{6}$

10. 7:4 or $\frac{7}{4}$

11. 2:3 or $\frac{2}{3}$

12. 3:4 or $\frac{3}{4}$

13. $p = 24$

14. $r = 3$

15. $n = 48$

Part Two
pages 31–32

1. $\frac{1}{5}$

2. $\frac{3}{5}$

3. $\frac{1}{3}$

4. $\frac{2}{5}$

5. $\frac{5}{7}$

6. $\frac{1493}{1500}$

7. $\frac{5}{7}$

8. $\frac{1}{1}$

9. (4) $\frac{5}{3}$

10. (4) $\frac{7}{3}$

11. (2) $\frac{3}{2}$

12. (3) $\frac{19}{12}$

13. (2) $\frac{1}{6}$

Part Three
pages 32–34

1. (3) $\frac{3}{5}$

3 of the five cards are face cards. Therefore, the probability of picking a face card is $\frac{3}{5}$.

2. (2) $\frac{1}{2}$

If you pick a face card the first try, 2 of the remaining 4 cards will be face cards. The probability of picking a second face card is then $\frac{2}{4}$, which reduces to $\frac{1}{2}$.

3. (3) $\frac{4}{3}$

For each 3 Plain Tacos sold, 4 Super Tacos are sold. Therefore, the ratio of Super Tacos to Plain Tacos is $\frac{4}{3}$.

4. (1) $\frac{1}{5}$

For each 10 tacos sold, 2 are Tacos Grandes. The probability of a customer ordering a Taco Grande is therefore $\frac{2}{10}$, which reduces to $\frac{1}{5}$.

5. (4) $\frac{8}{13}$

For each 2 Tacos Grandes sold, 4 Super Tacos are sold.

2 Tacos Grandes bring in
$2 \times $1.60 = 3.20

4 Super Tacos bring in $4 \times $1.30 = 5.20
The ratio of the money brought in by Tacos Grandes sales to the money brought in by Super Taco sales is thus $\frac{$3.20}{$5.20}$, which reduces to $\frac{8}{13}$.

6. (1) $\frac{3}{7}$

Out of each 10 tacos sold, 3 are Plain Tacos and 7 are not Plain Tacos. The ratio of Plain Tacos sold to other types sold is therefore $\frac{3}{7}$.

7. (5) 20

Let d = actual distance
Write a proportion of two equal ratios:
$$\frac{\text{actual distance}}{\text{map distance}} : \frac{d}{2\frac{1}{2}} = \frac{4}{\frac{1}{2}}$$

Solve for d: $d = \frac{4}{(\frac{1}{2})}(2\frac{1}{2})$

$$= 8(2\frac{1}{2}) = 20$$

8. (1) $3.84

Let c = cost of 8 heads.
Write a proportion of two equal ratios:
$$\frac{\text{cost}}{\text{number bought}} : \frac{c}{8} = \frac{$1.44}{3}$$
Solve for c: $c = \frac{$1.44}{3}(8) = 3.84

9. (3) $1.12
Let c = cost of 7 cookies.
Write a proportion of two equal ratios:
$$\frac{\text{cost}}{\text{number bought}} : \frac{c}{7} = \frac{\$1.42}{12}$$
Solve for c: $c = \frac{\$1.92}{12}(7) = \$1.12$

10. (1) $\frac{6}{8}$(20)
Let w = width of print
Write a proportion of two equal ratios:
$$\frac{\text{width}}{\text{length}} : \frac{w}{20} = \frac{6}{8}$$
$$w = \frac{6}{8}(20)$$

(The ratio $\frac{6}{8}$ has the same value if we change it to inches or leave it as feet.)

11. (4) (7)$\frac{(50)}{3}$
Let t = time to walk 7 miles.
Write a proportion of two equal ratios:
$$\frac{\text{time}}{\text{distance walked}} : \frac{t}{7} = \frac{50}{3}$$
$t = \frac{50}{3}(7)$, which can also be written $(7)(\frac{50}{3})$

12. (4) 16
If they won 4 for each 3 lost, Kristal's team won 4 out of each 7 games it played. Therefore, it won $\frac{4}{7}$ of its first 28 games.
$$\frac{4}{7} \times 28 = 16$$

13. (3) 65
Let x = number of chili sales Michael can expect. Write a proportion of two equal ratios:
$$\frac{\text{chilis sold}}{\text{hamburgers sold}} : = \frac{x}{260} = \frac{2}{8}$$
Solve for x: $x = \frac{2}{8}(260) = 65$

14. (1) $360
Out of each $.10 ($.04 + $.06) he invests, Mark puts $.04 in his savings account. He thus puts $\frac{\$.04}{\$.10} = \frac{4}{10}$ of the money he invests in his savings account. If he invests a total of $900, then $\frac{4}{10}$ of $900 is put in savings.
$$\frac{4}{10} \times \$900 = \$360$$

15. (3) 33
Of each 5 cars Brent sells, 3 are foreign made. Therefore, $\frac{3}{5}$ of all cars that Brent sells are foreign made.
$\frac{3}{5}$ of $55 = \frac{3}{5} \times 55 = 33$

16. (5) $\frac{48}{200}$(325)
Let h = height of taller building. Write a proportion of two equal ratios:
$$\frac{\text{building height}}{\text{shadow length}} : \frac{h}{325} = \frac{48}{200}$$
$$h = \frac{48}{200}(325)$$

17. (2) $(\frac{9}{4})$(7)
Let l = length of upper cable. Write a proportion of two equal ratios:
$$\frac{\text{length of cable}}{\text{bottom distance}} : \frac{l}{7} = \frac{9}{4}$$
$$l = (\frac{9}{4})(7)$$

PERCENTS
Part One
page 35

1. 32	10. 7%
2. 200	11. 3%
3. 105	12. 68%
4. 20	13. 16%
5. 221	14. $1304
6. 14	15. 28,300 voters
7. $190	16. $360
8. $7.50	17. 60 pickups
9. $84.50	

Part Two
pages 36–37

1. $27.30	11. 17%
2. $303.45	12. (2) 25%
3. $13,020	13. (2) 10%
4. 14 deaths per year	14. (4) 18%
5. $663.48	15. $42.50
6. $2.95	16. 27 people quit
7. $8112	17. $475.00
8. 4%	18. $640
9. 45%	19. $2280
10. 15%	20. (2) $26.25

Part Three
pages 37–39

1. (3) $2875
Amount due = principal plus interest
$$= 2500 + prt$$
$$= 2500 + (2500)(.20)(.75)$$
$$= 2500 + 375 = 2875$$

2. (3) $23.04
First price reduction:
20% of $36.00 = $7.20
1st sale price = $36.00 − $7.20 = $28.80
Second price reduction:
20% of $28.80 = $5.76
Purchase price = $28.80 − $5.76 = $23.04

3. (2) 10,032
Number of people voting: 64% of 28,500
64% of 28,500 = .64 × 28,500 = 18,240
Number of Democrats voting:
55% of 18,240
55% of 18,240 = .55 × 18,240 = 10,032

4. **(5) $72**
Original price of lamp: $120
1st sale price: $120 − ($\frac{1}{3}$)($120) = $80
Additional reduction: 10% of $80 = $8
Purchase price: $80 − $8 = $72

5. **(5) Not enough information is given.**
The problem says only that 25% of the ticket holders didn't show up. Nothing is said about what percent of the "stay at homes" were men or women.

6. **(4) $165**
The easiest way to solve the problem is to compute the interest that would be paid on a rate of 11%, the difference in the two interest rates.
$i = prt$
$i = ($1,500)(.11)(1)$
$ = 165

7. **(4) $\frac{(75 - 19)}{75}$**
Amount of race not completed = 75 − 19
Fraction of race not completed = $\frac{(75 - 19)}{75}$

8. **(2) (1 − .85)(12)**
The percent of teams that have not yet showed up = 100% − 85%.

Expressed as a decimal, (1 − .85) of the teams have not yet showed up.

This means that (1 − .85)(12) teams have not yet showed up.

9. **(2) $1250 + (.08)($1250)**
Manuel's salary increase = 8% of $1250
$ = (.08)($1250)$
Manuel's new salary
= original salary + salary increase
= $1250 + (.08)($1250)

10. **(1) $2220**
The least interest is paid to the company that requires the least total repayment money. Each total repayment is given below.
(1) $2220; (2) $2223; (3) $2256; (4) $2345; (5) $2360
Answer (1) is the smallest amount.

11. **(3) $155.65**
At Ben's, Chris receives a 15% discount and a $10 rebate. She does have to pay $5.00 for assembly and delivery.
Price at Ben's
$ = 189.00 − (.15)(189.00) − 10.00 + 5.00$
$ = 189.00 − 28.35 − 10.00 + 5.00$
$ = 155.65

12. **(1) $12\frac{1}{2}$%**
Percent decrease = amount of decrease divided by original price
$= \frac{24}{192} = .12\frac{1}{2} = 12\frac{1}{2}$%

13. **(3) the amount Value Hardware will charge for assembly**
The only cost that is not given is the amount Value Hardware will charge for assembly. We are told only that it is less than $15.

14. **(2) $2756**
Debbie needs $6200 minus the discount and minus the value of her trade-in:
Cash needed
$ = $6200 − 12% of $6200 − 2700
$ = $6200 − $744 − 2700
$ = 2756

15. **(4) $3510**
Trade-in offer = $2700 + 30% of $2700
$ = $2700 + 810
$ = 3510

16. **(5) Not enough information is given.**
To be able to answer this question, you must know how much of a cash discount the Chevrolet salesman will give.

MEASUREMENT
Part One
pages 40–41

1. 12	21. 365
2. 3	22. 16
3. 36	23. 2000
4. 5280	24. 1000
5. 1760	25. 100
6. 1000	26. 1000
7. 100	27. 4 ft
8. 1000	28. 18 jars
9. 16	29. 4 mi
10. 8	30. 20 oz
11. 2	31. 96 hr
12. 2	32. 75 ft
13. 4	33. 48 oz
14. 1000	34. 2 cups
15. 100	35. 2 m
16. 10	36. 650 g
17. 60	37. 124 mm
18. 60	38. 245 bottles
19. 24	39. 11 or 12 amp
20. 7	

Part Two
pages 41–42

1. 12 laps	9. 16 lb 4 oz
2. 14 trips	10. 11 hr 40 min
3. 5 hr	11. 88 km/hr
4. $14.00	12. 6 metric C
5. 3 hr 30 min	13. 290 g
6. 10 oz	14. 18 kg
7. 9:59 A.M.	15. 150 ml
8. 35 mi 1270 yd	

Part Three
pages 43–45

1. **(4) 3.2°F**
   Indicated temperature = 101.8°F
   Normal human body temperature 98.6°F
   The difference is found by subtraction:
   101.8°F − 98.6°F = 3.2°F

2. **(4) B and C only**
   Scale reading = $3\frac{6}{10}$ kilograms (kg).
   $\frac{6}{10}$ kg can be written as .6 kg or as 600 grams.
   $3\frac{6}{10}$ kg = 3.6 kilograms
   $\qquad\quad$ = 3 kilograms 600 grams

3. **(3) 6**
   Change the weight of each 1 pound 13 ounce bag to ounces only. Then multiply by 6 to find the total ounces.
   1 pound 13 ounces = 29 ounces
   29 ounces × 6 = 174 ounces
   Divide 174 ounces by 30
   $\frac{174 \text{ ounces}}{30}$ = 5.8 ≅ 6

4. **(2) 10:25 A.M.**
   Time Marquita placed call: 11:00 A.M. in Miami
   $\qquad$ 10:00 A.M. in Chicago
   Time Marquita hung up: 11:25 A.M. in Miami
   $\qquad$ 10:25 A.M. in Chicago

5. **(3) 6 gallons 1 quart**
   Total oil-based paint used during year
   = 25 × 6 = 150 gallons
   Total amount of paint thinner used = $\frac{150}{3}$
   = 50 pints
   Total number of gallons of paint thinner used = $\frac{50}{8}$ (since 8 pints = 1 gallon)
   $\qquad$ = 6 gallons 2 pints = 6 gallons 1 quart

6. **(5) 417,000**
   As indicated, the first meter reads in 100,000 cubic feet; the second in 10,000, and the third in 1,000.

7. **(4) A, C, B, D**
   For comparison purposes, change each weight to ounces only.
   $\qquad$ Bin A = 128 + 8 = 136 ounces
   $\qquad$ Bin B = 130 ounces
   $\qquad$ Bin C = 128 + 4 = 132 ounces
   $\qquad$ Bin D = 109 ounces
   From heaviest to lightest the order is A, C, B, D.

8. **(3) A, B, D, C**
   For comparison purposes, change each length to centimeters only.
   $\qquad$ A. 200 + 15 = 215 centimeters
   $\qquad$ B. 200 + 9 = 209 centimeters
   $\qquad$ C. 195 centimeters
   $\qquad$ D. 200 + 3 = 203 centimeters
   From tallest to shortest, the order is A, B, D, C.

9. **(4) 9:10 A.M. + 3 hours + 4 hours 45 minutes**
   When Jan leaves Seattle at 9:10 A.M., New York time is 3 hours later: 9:10 A.M. + 3 hours. The flight arrival time in New York is found by adding another 4 hours 45 minutes: 9:10 A.M. + 3 hours + 4 hours 45 minutes.

10. **(1)** $\frac{(36 + 8 - 9)}{7}$
    Lee starts with a piece 36 + 8 inches long. From this she cuts a 9-inch piece. She then has left a piece that is 36 + 8 − 9 inches long. This piece is divided into 7 equal-length pieces, each $\frac{(38 + 8 - 9)}{7}$ inches long.

11. **(5)** $\frac{(300 + 400 + 700 + 600)}{1000}$
    Total weight lost by Miklos in grams
    = 300 + 400 + 700 + 600
    Expressed in kilograms this weight
    = $\frac{(300 + 400 + 700 + 600)}{1000}$
    You divide by 1000 because it takes 1000 grams to equal 1 kilogram. The .5 kg (500 grams) weekly goal is not relevant.

12. **(2) 1.6**
    1 pound = 16 ounces
    10% of 1 pound = 10% of 16 ounces
    $\qquad\qquad\qquad$ = .10 × 16 ounces
    $\qquad\qquad\qquad$ = 1.6 ounces

13. **(3) 24%**
    Number of hours in a week: 24 × 7 = 168. Compute what percent 40 is of 168 by dividing 40 by 168. Round the answer to the nearest percent.
    $\frac{40}{168}$ = $.23\frac{136}{168}$ = 24%

14. **(5) between 6 and 7**
    1 deciliter = 100 milliliters.
    Number of tablespoons needed = $\frac{100}{15}$
    $\qquad\qquad\qquad\qquad\qquad$ = $6\frac{2}{3}$

15. **(1) 12 pounds 6 ounces**
    Total ounces needed: 18 × 11 = 198 ounces
    To change 198 ounces to pounds, divide by 16. $\frac{198}{16}$ = 12 pounds 6 ounces

16. (3) 32,436
On each of the first 4 dials, read the whole number the pointer has most recently passed: 3, 2, 4, 3, 6. The meter reads in kilowatt-hours, the dial at the right being the units dial.

GRAPHS AND TABLES
pages 46–55

1. 5 to 1 or $\frac{5}{1}$

2. food services worker

3. retail sales worker

4. (3) to the nearest $1000

5. by $96,000

6. (1) $\frac{1}{5}$

7. (5) 175%

8. (2) electronics repairman
School teacher salary = $20,000.
    30% of $20,000 = $6000
    $20,000 − $6000 = $14,000
Electronics repairman is the profession that earns $14,000.

9. (2) $\frac{1}{2}$ (22$\frac{2}{5}$ + 16$\frac{2}{5}$) (5000)
Add the two salaries and divide by 2—or, equivalently, multiply by $\frac{1}{2}$. The two salaries can be written as the total sum of the "$" symbols—counting each "¢" symbol as $\frac{1}{3}$ of a $— multiplied by 5000.

10. (5) Not enough information is given.
No information is given on the graph that enables you to conclude anything about the relative number of people employed in each profession.

11. 48%

12. 47%

13. $.26

14. $.31

15. $576

16. $528

17. $624

18. $192

19. (2) 3 to 1

20. (2) 2%

To determine the percent change, compute what part 100 is of 4800 and express the answer as a percent.
$\frac{100}{4800}$ = 0.02083 . . . ≈ 2.08% ≈ 2%

21. (2) **$1056**
Remembering that each cent represents 1% of the total budget, determine the three mentioned monthly costs:
Housing: 26% of $4800 = $1248
Transportation: 18% of $4800 = $864
Food: 22% of $4800 = $1056
To find the average, add the three costs and divide the sum by 3.
$\frac{\$1248 + \$864 + \$1056}{3}$ = $\frac{\$3168}{3}$ = $1056

22. (5) Not enough information is given.
No information is given that relates how much of the Turner family's transportation expenses depend on Darlene's job.

23. (2) **39%**
Brian's monthly income is $2304—48% of $4800. If he lost his job, but received $1200 each month in benefits, the amount of money he brings home would only decrease by $1104 ($2304–$1200).
Percent decrease in family income = $\frac{\$1104}{\$4800}$
= .23 = 23%

24. 1975

25. $340

26. $125

27. (2) $\frac{1}{3}$

28. (2) 25%
Percent increase = amount of increase divided by 1985 value
    = $\frac{(\$605 - \$480)}{\$480}$
    = $\frac{\$125}{\$480}$ = .260 . . . ≅ 25%

29. (4) 40%
Dorothy's 1990 monthly payments
    = $605 + $50
    = $655.
To find what part $262 is of $655, divide 262 by 655: $\frac{262}{655}$ = 40%

30. (4) $3025
Between 1970 and 1990, average benefits increased by a factor of 5 (a 400% increase). A fivefold increase between 1990 and 2010 would result in a payment in the year 2010 of 5 × $605 = $3025.

31. $109,000

32. 1980

33. (3) $41,000

34. (4) 5 to 1

35. (2) 25%
1990 price of an existing home = $96,000
1985 price of an existing home = $76,000
Increase in value: $96,000 − $76,000 = $20,000
Percentage increase = $\frac{\$20,000}{\$76,000}$
    = .263 . . . ≅ 25%

36. (4) $545,000
The price increase between 1970 and 1990 was nearly fivefold ($22,000 × 5 = $110,000). A fivefold increase between 1990 and 2010 would be $109,000 × 5 = $545,000.

37. $23 billion
38. 1981
39. 1970
40. (3) 24

41. **(2) 2 to 1**
1991 export value $\cong$ $40 billion
1991 import value $\cong$ $20 billion
Ratio of exports to imports $\cong$ $40 to $20
$= 2$ to 1

42. **(1) 33%**
Between 1985 and 1990, exports rose by approximately $10 billion; $40 billion (1990 value) $-$ $30 billion (1985 value) $=$ $10 billion. The percentage increase $=$
$\frac{\$10 \text{ billion}}{\$30 \text{ billion}} = .33 = 33\%$

43. 210 lb
44. 15 lb
45. 8 lb

46. **(4) $\frac{1}{7}$**
Body weight lost $= 210 - 180 = 30$ pounds
Fraction of total body weight lost $= \frac{30}{210} = \frac{1}{7}$

47. **(2) 6**
Average weight loss per month $=$ total weight loss divided by number of months of diet
$= \frac{30}{5} = 6$

48. 2 hr 11 min
49. Monday–Friday, 4:30 P.M.–7:30 P.M.
50. (4) 18 hr 15 min

51. **(2) 54 minutes**
In the table, locate the times that male and female teenagers watch TV on Sat. from 7 A.M. to 1:00 P.M. Compute the average by dividing the sum of these two times (49 minutes and 59 minutes) by 2.
$\frac{(49 + 59)}{2} = \frac{108}{2} = 54$ minutes

52. **(5) Not enough information is given.**
There is no Sunday-night-only time slot on the table. Therefore it is not possible to answer this question from information given on the table.

53. Rio de Janeiro, Brazil
54. New York, United States
55. (2) New York, United States
56. (5) 2.2 million

57. **(3) 30%**
São Paulo's population is projected to increase from 19.4 to 25.4 million, an increase of 6 million. The percent increase is
$\frac{6 \text{ million}}{19.4 \text{ million}} = .309 \ldots$ about 30%

58. **(2) Mexico City**
The projected population changes are as follows:
Tokyo—Yokohama
$30.0 - 27.5 = 2.5$ million
Mexico City
$27.9 - 21.6 = 6.3$ million
São Paulo
$25.4 - 19.4 = 6$ million
Seoul
$22.0 - 17.3 = 4.1$ million
Bombay
$15.4 - 12.5 = 2.9$ million

THE BASICS OF ALGEBRA

Part One
pages 56–57

1. e
2. g
3. f
4. a
5. h
6. d
7. b
8. c
9. $14 - n$
10. $5x$
11. $m + 32$
12. $\frac{20}{i}$
13. $9b$
14. $15 + r$
15. 8
16. 8
17. 24
18. 6
19. 6
20. 6
21. $690 + n$
22. $\frac{n}{8}$
23. $x + 5$
24. $\frac{2}{15}i$
25. No
26. No
27. Yes
28. No
29. 8 lunches
30. $1.58
31. 330 miles
32. 120 mph
33. $3\frac{1}{2}$ hrs
34. $2.38

Part Two
pages 57–58

1. $x = 38$
2. $y = 6$
3. $n = 6$
4. $y = 49$
5. $x = 1\frac{2}{3}$
6. $n = 6$
7. $6 + x = 14$
   $x = 8$
8. $x - 13 = 4$
   $x = 17$
9. $20x = 160$
   $x = 8$
10. $\frac{x}{4} = 9$
    $x = 36$
11. $x - 7 = 13$
    $x = 20
12. $3x = \$1.47$
    $x = \$.49$
13. $x - 25 = 34.95$
    $x = \$59.95$
14. $x = (\frac{2}{7})1470$
    $x = \$420$
15. $.06x = 507$
    $x = \$8450$
16. $x = \$72,000 + \$16,500$
    $x = \$88,500$
17. $x = 5$
18. $y = 9$
19. $c = 6$
20. $z = 1$
21. $x = 20$
22. $n = 48$
23. $x = 4$

24. $y = 5$
25. $n = 11$
26. 90 men
27. Stacey is 4.
 Shauna is 8.

28. $212
29. $420
30. $537.50

Part Three
pages 59–61

1. (4) 52
Let x = number of units sold, and set up an equation:
$550 + 14x = 1278$

Solve for x:
$14x = 1278 - 550$
$x = 52$

2. (2) 9
Let x = the smallest number.
$x + 1$ and $x + 2$ stand for the two larger numbers.

Set the sum of the three numbers equal to 30:
$x + (x + 1) + (x + 2) = 30$

Solve:
$3x + 3 = 30$
$x = 9$

3. (2) $3(d) + 2(2d) = 21$
Express each distance in terms of d:
Newman Park = d
City Reservoir = $2d$

Set the sum of total weekly distances equal to 21:
$3(d) + 2(2d) = 21$

4. (5) $\frac{4}{2.5}$
The correct ratio is written by placing what Mary receives above what Lillian receives, and then simplifying the ratio fraction.
$$\text{Ratio} = \frac{4.00}{2.50} = \frac{4}{2.5}$$

5. (4) 840
Paula earns $3.50 out of each $10.00 taken in. Paula's share, written as a fraction of the total, is thus $\frac{3.50}{10.00}$ or $\frac{4}{10}$.
Paula earns $(\frac{3.5}{10})(2400)$, or $840.

6. (1) $630 = \frac{4}{10}R$
Mary's share, $630, is equal to $\frac{4}{10}$ of R, the total receipts.

7. (1) $\frac{125}{(.02)(.75)}$
Solve the interest equation $i = prt$ for p:
$p = \frac{i}{rt}$

Put in the values for i, r, and t
$p = \frac{125}{(.02)(.75)}$, since 2% = .02 and
9 months = $\frac{9}{12}$ = .75 year.

8. (5) 47
Let x = the number of women, and $x + 19$ = the number of men. Write an equation:
$x + x + 19 = 75$

Solve:
$2x + 19 = 75$
$x = 28$

You are asked for the number of men:
$28 + 19 = 47$

9. (2) $\frac{3}{4}$ year
Use the interest formula, $i = prt$, and put in the values you know.
$22.50 = 1,000 \times .03 \times t$
$22.50 = 30t$
$\frac{3}{4} = t$

10. (4) $4,000 + (4,000)(.13)(\frac{7}{12})$
Compute the amount of interest owed after 7 months.
$i = prt = (4,000)(.13)(\frac{7}{12})$

To find the total owed, add principal and interest:
$4,000 + (4,000)(.13)(\frac{7}{12})$

11. (3) 53
To compute average speed, divide the distance by the time.
$\frac{212}{4} = 53$

12. (2) B only
The times are not needed if both the morning and afternoon distances are given.

13. (4) 117
The distance can be computed by multiplying the average speed by the time.
$d = (50)(\frac{7}{3})$, since t = 2 hr 20 min = $2\frac{1}{3}$ hr
$= \frac{7}{3}$ hr

14. (5) $848
Let x = monthly take-home pay, and set up an equation:
$\frac{1}{4}x = 212$

Solve:
$\frac{1}{4}x = 212$
$x = 212 \times 4 = 848$

The monthly rent is unnecessary information.

15. (2) 63
Let x = Mel's team's total points, and set up an equation:
$18 = \frac{2}{7}x$

Solve:
$18 \times \frac{7}{2} = (\frac{2}{7}x)\frac{7}{2}$
$63 = x$

The other team's points are unnecessary information.

16. (4) $89.00
To find the sale price of the bike, add Harry's final cost to the rebate.
74 + 15 = 89

You do not need the bike's presale price.

17. (2) $87
Let x = the amount Frank pays, x = the amount Scott pays, and $x - 75$ = the amount Jerry pays. Set up an equation:
$x + x + (x - 75) = 411$

Solve:
$3x - 75 = 411$
$3x = 486$
$x = 162$

The problem asks for Jerry's share:
$162 - 75 = 87$

18. (2) $1220
Let x = Mrs. Jameson's income and $1.5x$ = Mr. Jameson's. Set up an equation:
$x + 1.5x = \$3050$
$2.5x = \$3050$
$x = \$1220$

19. (2) 108
Let x = the number of people ordering pepperoni and $4x$ = number ordering sausage. Set up an equation and solve:
$x + 4x = 540$
$5x = 540$
$x = 108$

20. (5) $x(x + 17)$
Use the distributive law and separate out an x.

GEOMETRY
Part One
pages 62–64

1. $\angle C$
2. a. triangle
   b. rectangle
   c. cylinder
   d. cube
3. a. 3 mi 1040 yd
   b. 50 yd
   c. 132 m
4. 5
5. 8
6. 27
7. 100
8. $\frac{1}{9}$
9. 0.000016
10. a. 15 sq in
    b. 50 sq ft
    c. 1256 sq m
11. 468 sq ft
12. 15 sq yd
13. a. 90 cu in
    b. 1539 cm^3
    c. 125 cu ft
14. 63 cu ft
15. $3\frac{3}{8}$ cu yd
16. 3600 cu in
17. a. 37 degrees
    b. 50 degrees
    c. 138 degrees
    d. 50 degrees
18. 116 degrees

Part Two
pages 64–67

1. 145 ft
2. 186 sq in
3. 144 ft
4. 18
5. 23
6. 27
7. 34
8. 39
9. 43
10. 2.4
11. 7.1
12. 9.2
13. 7.7
14. 5.6
15. 10.5
16. $\frac{3}{4}$
17. $397.50
18. (3) 75 sq ft
19. (3) $\frac{1}{2}$
20. 12 truckloads
21. 400 cu yd
22. (3) 920 metric tons
23. e
24. a
25. b
26. d
27. c
28. (2) $\angle A = 73°$,
    $\angle B = 107°$,
    $\angle C = 73°$
29. (2) $\angle B = 58°$,
    $\angle C = 58°$
30. 210 ft
31. (4) $\triangle B$ and $\triangle C$
32. 10 mi
33. 14 ft
34. (3) 29 ft

Part Three
pages 67–71

1. (4) 5 mi
Find the circumference:
$2\pi r = 2 \times \frac{22}{7} \times 175 = 1100$ yd

Multiply by the number of laps:
$8 \times 1100 = 8800$ yd

Divide by the number of yards in a mile:
$8800 \div 1760 = 5$ mi

2. (5) 66 feet
Multiply the number of bricks by the length:
$88 \times 9 = 792$ in

Divide by the number of inches in a foot:
$792 \div 12 = 66$

3. (3) (2)(32) + (2)(18)
The sum of the sides is equal to twice the length plus twice the width.

4. (3) 150 feet
Divide the total area one can will cover by the height of the walls:
$400 \div 8 = 50$ ft

Multiply this length by the number of cans:
$50 \times 3 = 150$ ft

The volume of liquid in the can is unnecessary information.

5. **(3)** $\dfrac{(\frac{22}{7})(42)}{3}$

The approximate number is found by dividing the circumference by 3. The cirumference is 42 feet. π is represented by $\frac{22}{7}$.

6. **(1) 5 feet**
Use the Pythagorean relationship:
$c^2 = a^2 + b^2$
$c^2 = 3^2 + 4^2$
$c^2 = 25$
$c = 5$

7. **(3)** $\dfrac{6}{5}$
Find the two areas:
Patio = 270 sq ft
Garden = 225 sq ft

Write the ratio and reduce:
$\frac{270}{225} = \frac{6}{5}$

8. **(1) 10%**
Find the area of the whole backyard and the area of the patio:
Yard = 2700 sq ft
Patio = 270 sq ft

To find what percent 270 is of 2700, divide 270 by 2700:
$270 \div 2700 = .10$ or 10%

9. **(1) 2175 sq ft**
Subtract the area of the shed, garden, and patio from the area of the backyard:
$2700 - 30 - 225 - 270 = 2175$

10. **(5) 180 boxes**
Find the volume of the freezer:
$5 \times 3 \times 4 = 60$ sq ft

Convert box measurements to feet, and find the volume of one box:
12 in = 1 ft
4 in = $\frac{1}{3}$ ft
$1 \times 1 \times \frac{1}{3} = \frac{1}{3}$ cu ft

Divide freezer volume by box volume:
$60 \div \frac{1}{3} = 180$ boxes

11. **(2) 150**
To find the volume of the bed, convert inches to feet, and multiply:
8 in = $\frac{2}{3}$ ft
$V = (5)(\frac{2}{3})(6) = 20$ cu ft

Multiply the volume by the number of gallons per cubic foot:
$20 \times 7.5 = 150$

12. **(3) $48.86**
Find the area of the yard:
$28 \times 15 = 420$ sq yd

To find the number of bags needed, divide the area by the area one bag can cover.
$420 \div 30 = 14$ bags

Multiply bags by cost per bag:
$14 \times \$3.49 = \$48.86$

13. **(5)** $3.14(9^2 - 8^2)$
To find the volume of each inch of pipe, subtract the volume of the hole from the volume of a solid pipe with an 18-inch diameter:
$3.14(9^2) = 3.14(8^2)$

Use the associative law to rewrite $3.14(9^2) - 3.14(8^2)$ as $3.14(9^2 - 8^2)$.

14. **(4) The number of gallons in one cubic foot**

Since you know the number of cubic feet of water, the drainage rate in gallons per minute, and the time the draining starts, you need only know the number of gallons in each cubic foot. You can then determine the drainage rate in cubic feet per minute, find the time it takes to drain 15,400 cubic feet, and determine the time the pool will be empty.

15. **(3)** $c^2 - b^2 = 2^2$
The Pythagorean relationship says that the square of the hypotenuse is equal to the sum of the squares of the other two sides of a right triangle:
$c^2 = a^2 + b^2$

Fill in the side you do know:
$c^2 = 2^2 + b^2$

Subtract to get 2^2 alone on one side:
$c^2 - b^2 = 2^2$

16. **(2) E only**
$2^2 = 4$
$2^4 = 16$
$4^2 = 16$
$8^0 = 1$
$8^1 = 8$

17. **(5) 1728 cubes**
Find the volume of a box:
$12 \times 12 \times 12 = 1728$ cm^3

Find the volume of a sugar cube:
$1 \times 1 \times 1 = 1$ cm^3

Divide the volume of the box by the volume of a cube:
$1728 \div 1 = 1728$ cubes

18. **(3) the length of the tree's shadow**

By knowing this length, Frank can set up a proportion using the two measured shadow distances and the two heights—one of which he knows. He can then solve for the height of the tree.

19. **(3) C only**
A and B tell you something you can figure out anyway: the two triangles have the same 3 angles. To be congruent, though, the triangles must also be the same size, and choice C ensures that they are.

20. (5) $9^1 - 0^5$
$$3^2 - 2^0 = 8$$
$$9^0 - 1^4 = 0$$
$$4^2 - 3^2 = 7$$
$$3^3 - 5^2 = 2$$
$$9^1 - 0^5 = 9$$

21. (5) Not enough information is given.
Without knowing the length of at least one other side of the figure, you cannot find the area.

22. (3) 4 m
Find the area of the square:
$$8 \times 8 = 64 \ m^2$$

Since the rectangle has the same area, set up an equation with the numbers you already know:
$$64 = 16 \times w$$
$$4 = w$$

SPECIAL TOPICS IN ALGEBRA AND GEOMETRY

Part One
pages 72-73

1. 1	**14.** 30
2. -1	**15.** -21
3. F	**16.** 3
4. B	**17.** 61,837 ft
5. -1	**18.** 11°C
6. -4	**19.** 23°C
7. 7	**20.** 49 ft
8. 4	**21.** $x > 7$
9. 4	**22.** $n < 3$
10. -14	**23.** $z \geq -\frac{1}{2}$
11. 18	**24.** $7x \leq -6$
12. -7	**25.** $-4 \geq n$
13. -13	

Part Two
pages 73-74

1. (4) B, C, A, D	**11.** (4) $2^3 < 4^2$
2. 31°F	**12.** (1) 2
3. 197 lb	**13.** $12x^4$
4. $212.90	**14.** $2x^4y^3z^4$
5. $30.77	**15.** x^9
6. $n < 3$	**16.** $4c$
7. $z > 48$	**17.** $5\sqrt{2}$
8. $x > 10$	**18.** $5\sqrt{3}$
9. $y \leq 7$	**19.** $3\sqrt{5}$
10. (1) $-4 > -2$ is not true	**20.** $10\sqrt{5}$

Part Three
pages 75-77

1. (5) $x > 3n$
Let x = amount Ben will have in three weeks.
n = amount Ben has now
$3n$ = three times what Ben has now
According to the problem, $x > 3n$

2. (4) A and C only
On a number line, numbers get larger as you move from left to right.
A is true because M lies to the right of P and is larger.
C is true because N lies to the right of P but to the left of N.

3. (4) $F + 4 > 2(J + 4)$
The problem compares Fred's and Jimmy's ages 4 years from now.
Let $F + 4$ = Fred's age in 4 years
$J + 4$ = Jimmy's age in 4 years
$2(J + 4)$ = twice Jimmy's age in 4 years
According to the problem, $F + 4 > 2(J + 4)$

4. (3) A and D only
The computer sets off the alarm only when $n < 138$ (condition A) or when $n > 142$ (condition D). Choice C is in the acceptable range. Choice B itself does not set off the alarm unless choice D is true.

5. (2) $6(3x - 1)$
6 can be factored out of each term of $18x - 6$. Check the answer by multiplying:
$$6(3x - 1) = 6(3x) - 6(1) = 18x - 6$$

6. (1) $n^2(n - 8)$
n can be factored out of each term of $n^3 - 8n^2$. Check the answer by multiplying:
$$n^2(n - 8) = n^2n - 8n^2 = n^3 - 8n^2$$

7. (5) $8\sqrt{2}$
Let s = length of side of the square.
s^2 = area of the square = 128 square feet
To find s, take the square root of 128 and simplify the answer.
$$s = \sqrt{128}$$
$$= \sqrt{64} \cdot \sqrt{2}$$
$$= 8\sqrt{2}$$

8. (4) 36
Let x = width of lawn
$3x$ = length of lawn
The perimeter is found by adding all 4 sides.
$$\text{Perimeter} = 96 = x + 3x + x + 3x = 8x$$
$$96 = 8x$$
Solve for x and for $3x$.
$$x = \frac{96}{8} = 12$$
$$3x = 3(12) = 36$$

9. (1) 190

Let x = width of lot
$x + 25$ = length of lot
Perimeter = sum of 4 sides
$\qquad = x + x + 25 + x + x + 25$
$\qquad = 4x + 50$
Now set $4x + 50 = 810$ and solve for x.
$\qquad 4x = 760$
$\qquad x = \frac{760}{4} = 190$

10. (3) 3

Let b = base of triangle XYZ
$\qquad h$ = height of triangle XYZ

Area of triangle $XYZ = \frac{1}{2}bh = 9$

But the problem says $h = \frac{1}{2}b$. Replace h in area formula with $\frac{1}{2}b$. Multiply and then solve for b and h.

Area $= \frac{1}{2}b(\frac{1}{2}b) = 9$

$\qquad \frac{1}{4}b^2 = 9$

$\qquad b^2 = 36$

$\qquad b = \sqrt{36} = 6$

$\qquad h = \frac{1}{2}b = 3$

11. (4) $\frac{6}{1}$

Find the area of each rectangle.
$\qquad$ Rectangle II $= 2x3y = 6xy$
$\qquad$ Rectangle I $= xy$
Divide to find the ratio of area.

$\qquad \frac{\text{Rectangle II}}{\text{Rectangle I}} = \frac{6xy}{xy}$

$\qquad\qquad\qquad = \frac{6}{1}$

12. (4) (3,4)

Trying each point, you find that only (3,4) is not a solution to $y = 4x - 7$.
$\quad$ **(1)** $(1,-3)$ $\quad y = 4 \cdot 1 - 7 = 4 - 7 = -3$
$\quad$ **(2)** $(-2,-15)$ $\quad y = 4(-2) - 7 = -8 - 7 = -15$
$\quad$ **(3)** $(0,-7)$ $\quad y = 4 \cdot 0 - 7 = 0 - 7 = -7$
$\quad$ ***(4)** $(3,4)$ $\quad y = 4 \cdot 3 - 7 = 12 - 7 = 5$
$\quad$ **(5)** $(4,9)$ $\quad y = 4 \cdot 4 - 7 = 16 - 7 = 9$

13. (2) x intercept = 2 $\quad$ y intercept = 4

To find the x intercept, set $y = 0$ and solve for x:
$\qquad y = -2x + 4$
$\qquad 0 = -2x + 4$
$\qquad 2x = 4$
$\qquad x = 2$
To find the y intercept, set $x = 0$ and solve for y:
$\qquad y = -2(0) + 4$
$\qquad y = 4$

14. (3) 10

Use the distance formula to compute the distance between the points (3,3) and $(-3,-5)$.

$\quad d = \sqrt{\{3 - (-3)\}^2 + \{3 - (-5)\}^2}$

$\qquad = \sqrt{6^2 + 8^2} = \sqrt{36 + 64}$

$\qquad = \sqrt{100} = 10$

15. (2) $\frac{1}{2}$

Compute the slope by dividing the difference of the y coordinates by the difference of the x coordinates.

$\quad$ Slope $= \frac{3 - (-2)}{6 - (-4)}$

$\qquad = \frac{3 + 2)}{6 + 4} = \frac{5}{10}$

$\qquad = \frac{1}{2}$

16. (2) $x = 5, x = -1$

Trying each pair of x values, you find that only $x = 5$ and $x = -1$ solve the equation $x^2 - 4x - 5 = 0$.
$x = 5: 5^2 - 4 \cdot 5 - 5 = 25 - 20 - 5 = 0$
$x = -1 (-1)^2 - 4(-1) - 5 = 1 + 4 - 5 = 0$

17. (2) $y = 3, y = 4$

Trying each pair of y values, you find that only $y = 3$ and $y = 4$ solve the equation $y^2 - 7y + 12 = 0$.
$y = 3: 3^2 - 7 \cdot 3 + 12 = 9 - 21 = 0$
$y = 4: 4^2 - 7 \cdot 4 + 12 = 16 - 28 + 12 = 0$

18. (3) $\frac{4 - (-5)}{3 - (-2)}$

The slope is computed by dividing the difference of the y coordinates by the difference of the x coordiantes. The first coordinate in both dividend (top number) and divisor (bottom number) must be from the same point.

Formulas

Description	Formula
AREA (A) of a:	
square	$A = s^2$; where s = side
rectangle	$A = lw$; where l = length, w = width
parallelogram	$A = bh$; where b = base, h = height
triangle	$A = \frac{1}{2}bh$; where b = base, h = height
circle	$A = \pi r^2$; where π = 3.14, r = radius
PERIMETER (P) of a:	
square	$P = 4s$; where s = side
rectangle	$P = 2l + 2w$; where l = length, w = width
triangle	$P = a + b + c$; where a, b, and c are the sides
circle—circumference (C)	$C = \pi d$; where π = 3.14, d = diameter
VOLUME (V) of a:	
cube	$V = s^3$; where s = side
rectangular container	$V = lwh$; where l = length, w = width, h = height
cylinder	$V = \pi r^2 h$; where π = 3.14, r = radius, h = height
Pythagorean relationship	$c^2 = a^2 + b^2$; where c = hypotenuse, a and b are legs of a right triangle
distance (d) between two points in a plane	$d = \sqrt{(x_2 - x_1)^2 + (y_2 - y_1)^2}$; where (x_1, y_1) and (x_2, y_2) are two points in a plane
slope of a line (m)	$m = \frac{y_2 - y_1}{x_2 - x_1}$; where (x_1, y_1) and (x_2, y_2) are two points in a plane
mean	$mean = \frac{x_1 + x_2 + \ldots + x_n}{n}$; where the x's are the values for which a mean is desired, and n = number of values in the series
median	$median$ = the point in an ordered set of numbers at which half of the numbers are above and half of the numbers are below this value
simple interest (i)	$i = prt$; where p = principal, r = rate, t = time
distance (d) as function of rate and time	$d = rt$; where r = rate, t = time
total cost (c)	$c = nr$; where n = number of units, r = cost per unit